University of Nebraska Press

Lincoln and London

(Alt for Norge)

Translated and

with an afterword by

Conrad Røyksund

Pål Espolin Johnson

For Love of Norway

Originally published as
Alt for Norge
© J. W. Cappelens Forlag A/S,
Oslo 1975
Translation and afterword
copyright © 1989 by the
University of Nebraska Press
Library of Congress Cataloging-
in-Publication Date
Johnson, Pål Espolin, 1940-
[Alt for Norge. English]
For love of Norway /
Pål Espolin Johnson ;
translated and with an
afterword by Conrad Røyksund.
p.   cm. – (Modern Scandinavian
literature in translation)
Translation of: Alt for Norge.
ISBN 0-8032-2571-7 (alk. paper)
ISBN 0-8032-7571-4 (pbk.)
I. Title.
PT8951.2.046A7913   1989
839.8'2374 – dc19   89-5376 CIP

To Mother

Contents

1   Across the Bay at Mostad

5   Magda

10   Along House Brook Road

13   Barrels of Syrup and
Sermons for the Home

17   January 31

26   The Captain

30   Two Brothers

33   The Whole Community at Work

42   From the Dawn of Time

45   Twilight Time

49   Martines

56   Foggy Night

59   Where God Leads Me

63   Widow

69   For Love of Norway

78   A Hand to Hold To

83   Eagles and Brandy

90   English Daisies

96   "We'll Manage Somehow"

101   Full Sails

107   The Rescuer

112   With the Flag Held Low

117   The Bench

122   The Eighth Army

128   The Avalanche

131   Epilogue at the Fishing Hut

143   Afterword

Farthest out,

where the jagged Lofoten mountain range dives suddenly into the sea, lie the islands of Mosken, Værøy, and Røst.

By the steamship dock at Værøy – Rookery Island – there is a faded red fisherman's cottage, resting alone between the rocks and the racks for drying fish. It is there Magda lives.

What you are about to read is neither dream nor imagination: it is life itself as it once happened in an outlying Norwegian fishing village.

Magda, and all the others who told me the saga of Mostad, deserve my sincere thanks.

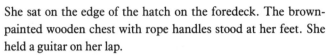

She sat on the edge of the hatch on the foredeck. The brown-painted wooden chest with rope handles stood at her feet. She held a guitar on her lap.

Out in the sea Mosken rose, black and steep, out of the morning haze. It ran toward the southwest, toward Rookery Island. The freighter pitched easily in the long, glistening swells. It was May 16, 1909.

He met her at Vågen. They put her wooden chest on the wheelbarrow. She wanted to carry the guitar herself.

Neither of them had ever been talkative. Only the sound of the iron wheel on the coarse gravel marked their way as they threaded through the shacks, and the racks used for drying fish.

They took the road. It began at Vågen and went inland toward Sørland. He went first with the wheelbarrow; she followed with the guitar.

Flat patches of meadow grass lay along the way, and a few houses. But behind the grass and houses there were only mountains, all around. The round, green-moss ridges and gray-pale crags lay with their faces toward the sea, stone protectors of the place.

There were signs of life behind some of the kitchen curtains as they passed. 'That must be her – Magda – who has come to live with Johan Nicholaisa.'

Johan's brother waited with the three-man boat at the bay in Sørland. That's where the men from Mostad left their boats when they landed. Two men always rowed when they went to

Sørland. The trip across the open bay at Mostad took a good hour. Vestfjord was open, and when the wind blew, men had to be strong.

Magda climbed in and sat on the aft thwart. Johan had laid his oilskins on the seat so she would not soil her travel clothes.

Then they pushed off and got underway. A thousand-foot mountain ridge pushed into the sea along one side of the bay at Sørland. Everyone called it Nupen. The ridge ended in a steep overhang they called Nuphetta – the Nob's Cap.

As soon as they rounded the point, they were in the bay. Johan and his brother bent their backs to the oars in earnest. With every stroke, a little tremor ran through Magda's back. And with every tremor, Mostad came a few fathoms nearer. The little white dots gradually became houses, and the houses got windows and doors and chimneys.

The beach changed, too. What had begun as a thin, even shoreline became a chaos of huge boulders. Only a few dark channels opened up between the masses of rocks. They were the landings that led to the sod-roofed boathouses.

It was the mountain that changed most. From the other side of the bay it had looked like a lazy lion resting on the surface of the sea. A majestic lion with his proud head facing south; his back arched north. But when they came in toward shore, the side of the lion became a vertical wall of cliffs and crevices. The long reach of mountain blocked off everything south and west along the whole length of the little village, sinking both the small cluster of houses and the people along the shoreline into shadow, even though it was early in the day, and May.

A pack of cranky dogs objected furiously as the boat glided into the landing. The children playing along the shoreline dropped whatever they were holding and ran to see what was happening. Oluf Berntsa stood by the boathouse tending his boat. He straightened up, nodded, and greeted them as they landed.

He still stood there as they left, mumbling to himself: Well, well! He often said Well, well! when there was something going on. Johan had brought an elegant woman home from Lofoten.

He watched her as she climbed the path, she and her guitar, as straight as a ramrod. And tall. About as tall as Johan. Nothing wrong with her clothes. Her newly knitted stockings shone white beneath her variegated gray coat, and her hat was black, banded with a red ribbon.

Johan's father, Edvard, stood in suspenders at the door to greet them, and asked how the trip had gone. His mother sat on a stool in a corner by the stove.

Maren. Edvard and Maren. She took Magda's hand in her own arthritic grasp. But as she welcomed Magda she noted everything, from the shoelaces in the newcomer's city shoes to the band around her broad-brimmed hat. Crippled or not, Magda thought, the control of this house still lies behind those old brown eyes of the woman on that stool.

After coffee and something to eat, Magda climbed to the loft. Johan had set the wooden chest on the floor over by the window.

The shoreline was just a few yards from the house. And the bay. Farther in, at the head of the bay, lay a low neck of land. From there, and all down the other side of the mountain, was a long, sky-high ridge, hiding Sørland to the east.

From Nupen south, the mountain was a stone, saw-toothed ridge. First there were the great molars, and farther out, the stone teeth, worn down. Finally, as the ridge met the sea, only the gums remained.

Magda opened the wooden chest. It was large and festive, the work of a careful craftsman. It wasn't just a glued and nailed box. Everything had been carefully dovetailed. The outside corners of the trunk had been reinforced with metal, and the inside was warm with lovely birch. There was even a covered tray in it.

She stood there a moment, looking at the chest, running her hand over the finely planed lid on the tray. Her brother had built it for her. Leander, who had died at sea. It had been the last chest he had made before he had shipped out in a sealing ship. They had shipwrecked in a hurricane on their way to Iceland. There was never a sign of either the boat or the crew.

Magda opened the tray and took out a small box. Leander had bought the brooch for her while he had been in Bergen once on a small sailing cargo ship. They were almost the same age. None of the others had as much in common as they. She had lost both a brother and a friend.

***

On top, in the main part of the chest, was the book her mother had given her: 'Follower of Christ,' her mother had written. 'Read this carefully. It will be your guiding star.'

But beneath the book and her diary and other little mementos lay her work clothes. She took off her travel clothes and put on her blue dress. She stuck her bare feet into her clogs and climbed back down. Evening found her sitting at the sewing machine.

She came from a place at the foot of the mountains, far out on the Lofoten peninsula. She had been born on July 29, not just a Sunday, but St. Olaf's day.

Four families lived in Tuv. Their houses were yellow, and lay squeezed together between some knolls and the boulders on the beach. They had neither a road nor a harbor, and offshore the Mosken current ran hard and fast.

But behind the houses, a field of grass ran up the hillside. Up where the hill leveled off, there was a meadow with a large lake. Beyond the meadow a wide and fertile valley pushed up into the mountains. Along both sides, patches of grass as green as weathered copper reached up between the ridges.

Magda's childhood kingdom was among these mountain meadows. She had food, and her own bed, a mother and a father and brothers and sisters in the house down by the sea, but it was up in the valleys where she lived. *Really* lived.

From the time she had barely been old enough, she had stayed at home and taken care of the younger children when her older sister and parents went up into the valleys to do the haying. She managed to sit there by their cradles, day after day, for the first few years. The children came close together in their home. Often, when her parents came home from the haying, they found everyone asleep at the cradles; the babies inside, and Magda nodding over the side.

When she was old enough to hold a rake handle, a younger sister was assigned to child care. Then it was Magda's turn up in the valley. From the time she had been confirmed, she had carried hay down to the house, like an adult. From that time on, she gladly stayed up in the valley the rest of the summer, too, tended the animals, and was her own boss. Whenever the cows wandered up onto the steep hillside, she ran to turn them down again, so that they would not get lost and stranded.

Magda was so good at herding that no one ever took the job from her. From June until September, year after year, she wandered around with the little herd of cows. In midsummer, she ran barefooted from grass patches to clumps of young birches, wearing only a little tattered dress.

A meadow with a lake, a grass-covered hillside, and a herd of cows against a towering Lofoten mountain: that was Magda's world. For her, it was a delightful world. She could not imagine anything better than being up in the valley. And even if there was so much to be responsible for, it was a free life.

In wintertime the men went fishing and came home only on weekends. The women lived indoors. Magda had her chores to do in the barn, but otherwise she sat in the kitchen, doing weaving and sewing. When they needed clothing, they had to make it themselves. Everything from their underclothing to the things they slept in. It took a lot to keep eleven children clothed.

But winter was not just indoor life. As soon as the ice had formed on the lake up in the valley, the children were on their way up. The boys had skates they had made from pieces of birch and scraps of tin. They pushed off and made wonderful loops and circles on the clear ice. The girls found someone's belt to hang onto, and swung around at the side, their skirts sweeping the ice.

Sofie and Lauritz were strict parents. Their motto was Obedience in the Home. Quarreling was forbidden. Everyone knew the switch stood behind the door. And there were more birch rods at the south side of the house. It was there that Lauritz always got a new supply.

Every night there were prayers and hymns. No one ate until the table grace had been said. It was the duty of the oldest child to begin the prayer; the others joined in as well as they could.

There was no school in Tuv. If the children were to receive any education at all, they had to be rowed to Evenstad or Helle, miles away. But Lauritz began their education at home. Before Magda had been rowed to school for the first time, she had learned both to read and to write. Their father started them a year early, and gave them lessons as strictly as any schoolteacher. When they didn't know a lesson, they had to go up to the loft and stay there until they had learned it.

Magda went to school for seven summers. That was six weeks in early summer, and six more in late summer. She stayed in the loft of some people they knew, and came home for a break after the first six weeks. Every once in a while, someone rowed in from Tuv with a packet of food and some clean clothes.

She had a new teacher each year. The seventh and the last of them came from down south, and was named Henriksen. He was a noncommissioned officer, and a bachelor, and stricter than all of the others put together. But Magda was a good student. Only once, that whole year, did she not know her lesson. The old soldier was reasonable enough to give her a chance to know it by the next day. That night Magda locked herself into the room in the loft and sat there the whole night, learning what she had to know.

On the last day of school she was called up to the teacher's desk and received her diploma. It was edged in gold, and had a

7

colored picture of a costumed girl holding a bouquet of flowers. For Demonstrated Diligence and Attention in School, it said in ornate handwriting.

There were three young girls in Tuv. They tried to meet every Sunday evening. Magda's mother used to sing old folk songs when she sat at the spinning wheel and spun wool. Magda had learned her mother's songs, and taught them to her friends in the evenings when they met together.

On her eighteenth birthday, she received a guitar from an uncle. He had bought it in Bodø for eighteen kroner. The fishing had been good that year. Magda had never played the guitar, but she learned fast, and soon the girls were both singing and playing music on Sunday evening.

On Midsummer's Night all of the young people who were home for the summer got together up at the lake. The girls picked blossoms and made wreaths of flowers for their hair, while the boys watched and tried to look like men. And it was like that – all of them singing – that they came up to the mountain. They climbed to the top of Hellsegga and watched the sun on the shortest night of the year. The view from almost two thousand feet was beautiful. On the west, the ocean stretched as far as they could see. Toward the south Mosken and Rookery Island stuck up out of the sea, and farthest out shined the bird rookeries on Røst.

But not everyone went up to the mountain on Midsummer's Night. That was only for grown-ups. No one was allowed to climb to Hellsegga who had not been confirmed by the pastor.

***

It happened in Tuv, as it did in other places, that young people fell in love in summer, when the days were longest and the nights were bright with the midnight sun. But not so for Magda. She could be friends. With anyone. From anywhere: Hell or Å or Evenstad. But not fall in love. Magda was careful about that.

It was an accordion that brought Magda and Johan together. Leander, her brother, played for a dance in Å one Saturday night. Johan came. He had been doing construction work, and was ready to go home again.

Johan could play the accordion a little. He met Leander, and they talked. When the dance was over, he went home with Leander to Tuv. And there he met Magda.

After that, letters began to cross between the Lofoten peninsula and Rookery Island. After a year had passed, an engagement ring came in the mail to the post office in Tuv.

In the spring, Johan's sister was going to be confirmed. Her mother had arthritis and could not sew a confirmation dress. Johan wrote to Magda, and Magda packed her things and came.

When she had finished the confirmation dress, she began to sew Johan's bridal shirt. The wedding was to be in July, at the Valhalla Cafe in Kabelvåg. The bridal dress was high-necked, and black, but over that large head of brown hair there was to be both a white veil and a green wreath. She rented the rest of her trousseau from a shop in Kabelvåg. The shop owner herself dressed her.

It happened that on the day of the wedding, Magda's cousin came north on the steamship. He had been in America, and had saved money for several years. He borrowed a fiddle, and played for the procession, both into and out of the church.

At home in Mostad, the newly married couple was given a room in the loft. It was light green, and newly painted, and had a

9

bed, a table, and a washstand. The pitcher and the washbasin were a wedding present from Johan's father.

Magda became responsible for the care of the whole house. Normally there were seven of them, and in the winter, ten. Johan was the skipper of a fishing boat, and had hired men boarding with him during the fishing season. And out in the barn, there were twelve sheep and a cow.

That is how Magda came to Mostad on Rookery Island. She was twenty-five years old.

Along House Brook Road

Actually, Magda had been in Mostad once before. At the time she had thought to herself that she could never live in such a bare and depressing place.

Twenty families crowded together on a patch of grass between the mountain and the sea: that was Mostad. A hundred and twenty human beings thrown to the mercy of fish and birds and weather and water. No one knew for certain how long people had lived in the little fishing outpost. Some remembered that the pastor had said something about the thirteenth century. He was supposed to have read that in one of his books.

It made no difference. Whether Mostad had been founded before or after the plague made life neither better nor worse. But what they did know was that not everyone in Mostad spoke with a northern dialect. Many of them had come from western Norway, down south. They had come up in the 1870s and settled down. That was how the neighborhood had filled up. They had come to make a living. Things were worse down south. In Mostad there was food: birds in the mountains, and the sea and fish were near. In Mostad, as they saw it, one could both survive and live.

On the map it said 'Mostad,' but in Mostad they called it the Mostad Homestead or, preferably, just the Homestead. The houses were so close together that they were almost all in a cluster. There were neighbors who had just a few yards of space between them. They told about a young fellow who had both proposed and been accepted through the attic window of his house. The girl had stood in her nightgown in the window of the house next door.

And down by the shoreline, the boathouses stood shoulder to shoulder, leaning for support against each other.

There was only one road in Mostad. It ran from north to south through the middle of the field and was about a quarter of a mile long. At the north end there was a white building with tall windows and a flagpole. That was the schoolhouse. The spring, or the house brook, as they called it, was at the other end. It was the only source of water in Mostad. There were always women with wooden yokes to be seen along the road, and that is why they called it the House Brook Road. They carried water for washing and cooking; for the animals and for people. House Brook Road was the only conveyer belt in Mostad.

One often walked the road many times a day. Magda was one of those who had the longest way to go. She lived at the north end of the Homestead, almost at the school. When night came, and she hung the yoke up for the night, she had made eight or ten trips with her buckets. And tramped at least three miles.

Everything from the road up to the foot of the mountains was the women's world. It was they who took care of the animals in the small sheds, and it was they who planted the potatoes in the tiny patches in back of the sheds, and who dug them up when fall came.

The men worked below House Brook Road when they were not at sea or up in the mountains. Down there were the boathouses and the sheds for gear and the drying racks, the boats and the boat landings. Down there were the five-man boats and the longlines they spent all winter with. Through most of the rest of the year they fished with handlines. Then they used the smaller boats: the two- and three-man boats. Two men could handle them. If they had a son growing up, they could take him along and save themselves the price of a hired man. The boys could hold the boats steady while their fathers fished.

The men at Mostad were noted for the good condition of their boats. And no one wanted to ruin their reputation. During the summer, there was always someone tarring or repairing or painting. They were especially careful with the colored stripe along the gunwale. First a broad white border, then a narrow black stripe, and then a really good, broad green field. Then a narrow white stripe and a still narrower reddish brown one. A newly tarred and newly painted boat coming out of the harbor at Mostad was something of a floating painting, lying there, reflecting off a smooth sea.

Even when they did not have to, the men willingly went down to the shore. If there was nothing to work on, there was always something to talk about. Down by Martinus Torstensa's boat-house there was a patch of ground that was packed as hard as glass. They called it the Heap. It was there they stood with their hands in their pockets and with their heads together. The kids knew that when they stood like that it was best to stay away. If they came up then, squeezed in through the circle of legs, and said, 'Papa!' they knew what kind of an answer they would get: 'Go home to your mother!'

 *Barrels of Syrup and Sermons for the Home*

The little, light blue enameled sign on the inside of the door read: NORDLY'S ROASTED COFFEE, Wilhelmsen's Blend. Up over the counter there was a sign for TROMSØ MARGARINE.

The store was at the north end of the Homestead, up by the school, and was open whenever Petter Kristensa, the owner, felt like it. The yellow-painted building was long and narrow. It lay on the lower side of House Brook Road with its gable toward the sea. The front of the store had three high windows and a double door with stone steps leading in. Inside there was an entryway, the shop itself, and a small office with a tall writing desk where Petter used to stand and keep his books.

Petter was a powerfully built man. He was strong enough to carry two-hundred-twenty-pound barrels of syrup. He always wore overalls, and had a broad leather belt around his waist. A large knife in a sheath hung from the belt.

He was bald on top, but around the edges his hair was stiff and brown. His beard was so thick that his younger children used to hide their faces in it when he bent over their beds to tell them good night. It was so nice and warm in there. And Petter himself used to say that there was no better cure for a toothache than to snuggle one's cheek up into his beard.

Petter's white, two-storied house stood proudly just up the hill from the store. It had a big porch and wide steps down toward the road. When the people in Mostad had shopping to do, they usually had to go up the steps to the house to find him. Or else go down to the boathouse by the bay and find him there.

He seldom sat around with his hands in his lap, doing nothing, unless it was Sunday. Petter was a glutton for work. If there was no one in the store, he closed the door and went down to the shore and worked with the fish. He was the buyer who took the fish to Bergen and resold it. Most of the preparation of the fish he did himself. When he split the fish he sat right in the middle of the boathouse on a plank he had laid over a washtub, surrounded by a heap of cod and pollack, splitting and slicing with the knife he had made from a broken scythe blade. He had made the wooden handle, too.

In spring, the wall of the little country store was covered with fish hanging out to dry, protected by netting. And what he could not hang on the store wall, he hung down by the beach under the boathouse. The birds got a few of the fish, and the dogs got a few more. But there were always some left over and, late in the summer, he got people together to load the five-man boat. When it was all stacked on board, he climbed up to the top of the mountain of dried fish and sat down. He sat that way while they rowed him across the inlet, around Kvalnes, and into Vågen. There everything was loaded onto a small cargo boat for the trip south.

He was usually gone for a month or so. He came home with supplies for the store for the whole year. Bolts of homespun, sacks of sugar, sewing thread and fishhooks, barrels of syrup and chewing tobacco.

There was always excitement among the children in Petter's household when the cargo boat from Bergen was expected to arrive back up north again. If Petter had gotten a good price for the fish, there might be both brooches and velvet for a new dress.

Petter seldom came back from Bergen without something for the house. He lived for auctions when he was down south. He was a modest man and didn't think it made any sense to buy something new when something used was available. His living room was filled with furnishings from bankrupt homes in Bergen. In the middle of one wall there was a black lacquered buffet with a big soup tureen on top. There were mirrors in the doors of the cabinet. Inside, on the shelves, there were two sets of dinnerware. One white and delicate, and the other with flowers and a gold rim.

Over on the south wall there was an organ he had brought home one year. It had been terribly difficult to bring it ashore and up to the house, and Petter had given up trying to learn to play it. It just stood there now, and looked rather nice, at that.

The most fun had been the year he came with the brass lamp. It was the shiniest thing they had ever seen, and larger than any of the other lamps in Mostad Homestead. When Petter lighted the lamp on special occasions, the other Homesteaders enjoyed strolling north just to stand in the road and admire its glitter and shine.

One year he came north with a long-stemmed pipe for himself. It had been given to him by the fish buyer in Bergen. The pipe had a lid made of genuine silver, and was so elegant that he took it down from its place on the wall only once a year. That was on Christmas Eve.

He didn't smoke otherwise, but on Christmas Eve he tamped it full and lit up. He scattered tobacco incense about the fireplace hearth, and sat in the rocking chair, puffing and presiding over the holiday.

★★★

It was easiest to find him in the store in the evenings, when he had received the day's fish and was through with the outside work. He often sat at a bench behind the counter, repairing shoes. The women had usually done their shopping earlier in the day. Evenings, it was the men's turn, and they came mostly just to talk.

In a corner by the door, the younger boys sat in a clump and soaked up every word the grown-ups said. Petter subscribed to the *Lofoten Post*, and generally had important things to report.

Two walls of the store were covered with shelves and drawers. Over in the corner there was a round stove as tall as a man. Behind the counter, there was a steep stairway that went up through a hole in the ceiling. It was up there that Petter had his storehouse. It was a happy boy who got to go up there with Petter. It was a twilight adventure world filled with bags and barrels and boxes and bundles. And over everything there lay the fragrance of tar and tobacco and spices.

Petter loved children. He loved to talk to them when they came on errands for their mothers. And when they left, he licked his huge thumb and ran it across their mouths: "I am going to give you a licking," he said. And then he chuckled so hard that his knife jiggled at the back of his overalls, and his eyes became wrinkled slits in his bearded face.

It was his way of telling the children that he liked them.

★★★

And while Petter was a shopkeeper and fish buyer, he was also a man who took his Lord seriously. Every day of the year he held evening devotions at dinnertime. No one left the table until Petter had read a sermon from the book and they had sung a hymn. And no one read the Psalms other than he, either. The Psalms were to be memorized. And it was Petter's conviction that one did not learn to memorize by looking at the book.

The people in Mostad thought that Petter was a good and fair merchant. He was never able to say no when they didn't have any money and were in need of something. He was like one of *them*. He had himself been a fishing boat captain and a fisherman. One time he had sailed across the keel of an overturned boat, and saved two men from drowning.

Petter knew fishing too well to turn his back when they came to him and needed something.

There were three classes of people in Mostad. There were those who owned land, those who did not own land, and Petter, who owned both a store and land.

After Petter, those who owned land did best. If they had a little patch of soil on their land, they could raise potatoes. If they had a field up in the mountains, they could own animals, and get milk and meat and wool.

The others in Mostad did the best they could. Magda and Johan were among them. They had to rent land in order to have animals.

There were those who came to Mostad so late that there was not even land to be rented. That is what happened to Anna and Oluf Tuv. They came about the turn of the century, and had built a shack down by the shoreline, about as far south as it was possible to live in the Homestead. There wasn't any grassy level space left. A narrow, rugged strip between the shore and the boulders broken loose from the mountain was all there was. It was there they had squeezed their house in, between the boulders and the rocky mounds.

The sea was so close that when the tide was high and there was a storm, their house was sprayed with salt water. Sometimes seaweed would come flying through the air and plaster up against their windows. Regularly, during the fall, Anna made her rounds with a washcloth and wiped the salt from the windowpanes so they could see out. No one lived in a more exposed situation.

No one saw less of the sun, either. The mountain – Tinden – hung over them and cut off the light. Nowhere in Mostad did the shadows come earlier in the morning than they did over the house of Anna and Oluf, down at the south end.

The house was gray and unpainted, and there was not much of anything inside. In the living room there was a piece of outdoor furniture Oluf had won in a lottery one year while winter fishing. It was white and had iron feet. There was a tinted picture on the wall behind the bench. It showed the newlyweds standing before the pastor at the altar. An angel stood on each side guarding them.

Mostly, they lived in the kitchen. There was a little couch in there where they could stretch themselves out. They each had a stool, and an oilcloth-covered table to sit at. One window looked over the bay, and another up toward the mountain. Over in one corner, the stairs disappeared up into the loft.

But even though Anna did not have much, what she did have was orderly. The unpainted plank floor was scoured with sand, and the bleached wooden walls glistened and smelled of soap. What there was of wooden containers and ladles, of cups and bowls, hung scrubbed and shiny down the wall. Or else they stood neatly deployed along the bench and in the tiny cupboard. In Anna's house, everything had its place.

No one at the Mostad Homestead was as poor as Anna and Oluf. All the land they had was the piece the foundation for the house stood on, and even that was not theirs. They did not have any animals, and even if all they needed was a cup of milk, they had to walk to the Homestead for it. They always owed money to Petter. But they had to get food somehow. They had four children.

Anna struggled and toiled, as much as Oluf, to find a way to make ends meet. People brought her bags and containers of sheep's wool. From early in the morning until late at night she sat at the spinning wheel in the kitchen. Straight-backed, and short and round as a butterball. Her hair was as black as coal, and her braids lay in coils at her neck.

Most of the wool in Mostad became yarn in Anna's hands. But the income wasn't much. She could not bring herself to take much pay for what she did.

★★★

It happened one winter, at the end of January. Anna and Oluf and the children sat around the table eating their dinner. Together with a hired man from Borge who had come to live with them during the Lofoten fishing season. Their youngest child – sixteen weeks old – lay in the cradle. Anna had given birth to her fourth child in the fall.

There had been a heavy storm for several days. The men had had to pull their boats ashore. Like the other men, Oluf was impatient to get to sea. While they were sitting there by lamplight, they suddenly heard a thunderous noise up in the loft. It was as if something heavy had fallen to the floor. 'The longline gear must have fallen down,' Oluf said, and got up and went up the steps. But everything looked all right. The gear was still in its place. 'What is this all about?' he wondered as he came back down.

As the night went on, the wind died down, and already, before the dark of night had loosed its grip in the morning, the five-man boats were afloat, all the gear on board.

They rowed out in the gray morning light. For three days they had been lying ashore. The men raced down the bay. They were headed for the Outer Bank, south in the Røst Sea. It was a long way to row, but the fishing was a little better there.

It was January 31, 1910.

★★★

Magda had just had twins, and had not been outdoors since the birth. She sat at the kitchen table fixing clothing for the new babies. She had not counted on there being two of them.

Later in the morning, the first blast of wind hit hard against the north wall. It came as if let loose from a sack. In hardly more than a moment, Mostad Homestead was encompassed by a snowstorm so thick that they could not see from one house to the next.

Forty men had rowed out in the morning. There was no one left on land except the women and the children, and here and there a few old fellows too old to be at sea. Every house had a father at sea. And most of the fathers had sons with them in the boats.

Magda was uneasy. Johan's whole crew lived in her house. There were five men on board. And Johan's father was fishing in a small boat with some other old fellows in Vågen.

She pulled on a man's jacket that hung out in the entryway, and tried to go over to the neighbors, just to hear what they thought over there. But the door to the entry was stuck, and would not move. The wind was so strong that she could not push it open, so she gave up and went back in.

Maren sat, as she usually did, in her corner by the fireplace, trying to fold her two arthritic hands in the lap of her apron. In the cradle, the twins lay sleeping, head to foot.

The weather got worse as the day wore on. The house shook in the worst blasts of wind. Magda rarely left the bedroom window. Out on the bay, the snow and the spray were mixed together. Despite the offshore wind, the sea was heavy.

In mid-afternoon, there was a lull between gusts in the storm. Magda was able to see the figures of three women hunched together, setting out up House Brook Road in coats and kerchiefs.

Then she realized how seriously wrong things were. They were headed out toward the headland. She knew that native-born Mostad women did not go out there in the winter without good reason! When they headed out in that direction, to stand there beneath that huge, bare rock in the middle of a storm, it was because they were deathly afraid. They went out there to sit just to be able to see a few yards out on the ocean in the direction of Røst Sea. They knew that if the men were ever to find land again, they would have to come from that direction.

It grew late, and the day began to darken. Just as despair began to seep into Magda, she heard a shout from Iver Ellingsa's house, down below. She ran to the bedroom window and saw that there were boats and men down at the shore.

Two five-man boats had managed to row up beneath the mountain, and into the bay. Ten exhausted men stumbled around the boathouse, trying to secure the boats and the gear on land.

There was relief in a few houses, but the anxiety rose in the others. The men who returned had rowed through wreckage. They had seen oars and longline tubs in the sea.

During the night, the wind died down. At a break between two squalls, there was life at still another boat landing. It was Georg and his crew. But they did not have much to say about the other Mostad five-man boats. They had seen neither men nor boats. It had been all they could do to bail and manage the sails and lines in their own boat.

***

Georg and his men had been setting their gear when the storm broke. The weather had still been good as they had set the first tub of gear. But then they saw that it was beginning to storm off the snow-covered peak of Mostad. They realized the wind was picking up.

They had a tub of gear for each of the five men on board. But by the time they had set the fourth, the wind had become so strong that they could not continue.

They set themselves to rowing. It didn't do much good. They were headed right into the wind. Rowing as hard as they could, they never moved from where they were. As one stroke of the oars drove them forward, the storm drove them back even before they could get their oars back into the water for the next stroke. The wind caught the oar of the man in the bow, tore it up from the oarpin, and smashed it into the head of the man sitting in the middle. There was only one thing they could do: try to get the mast up and begin to sail. It was not much of a sail they hoisted. They had to be careful not to capsize the boat. 'We have to be careful,' said Georg, who sat astern, and was the skipper. 'Sooner or later, the wind has to die down.'

They began to tack back and forth. They were kept busy. They kept shipping water over the side, however careful they were not to let out much sail. Up in the bow, Nikolai sat in his leather pants, shouting warnings to them of breakers and dangerous waves that came up suddenly. Peder sat on the middle thwart and tended the line that held the sail, and in the stern Johan bailed the boat as fast as he could with the big wooden scoop.

First they were driven east, deep into Vestfjord. When they tried to change direction, they had to get the oars out to try to help. But that didn't work either, and they had to come about. They ran west toward Røst. But in Røst Sea the waves caused by the current and the wind were so heavy, and the breakers so dangerous, that they had to come about again and sail east, back toward the fjord and away from Mostad and Rookery Island. If they gained a little in one tack, they lost it in the next.

The last time they were in near Rookery Island, the day had gone so long that it was getting dark and difficult even to see the waves. Then the whole wild storm hit them all at once again, so hard that they had to take the sail down altogether. Georg shouted to Peder, who was tending the sail line, and the sail slammed down to the seat. There was nothing to do but wait until the wind abated.

They were freezing. They had been wet the whole day, and there had not been time to think of food. For ten hours they had chased back and forth across a wild sea, trying to save the boat and their own lives, even though the shred of sail they had up was not big enough for the crossbeam to be out of reach when they stood on the middle thwart. Now they had to try to see if they had enough strength left to row up to Mostad.

They took their oars, and set out to row in the dark. Finally, somewhere up by the bay at Mostad, there was a little break in the weather, so that they could haul themselves into land. It was nine o'clock at night; fifteen hours since they had rowed out.

★★★

It had become quiet after the storm, late in the evening, when Magda dressed to go out to the barn to take care of the animals. She had seen nothing of Johan. Only three of the eight boats had returned to land. Still more of the women had trudged out to the headland. They sat in a knot and stared out at the black winter night. Magda had to stay at home. There were the twins to care for.

As she came from the barn, and was about to go into the house again, she heard someone moaning and crying down in the Homestead. Two men led a woman south along the shore.

Johan was standing in the kitchen taking off his clothes when she came in. He and another fellow had rowed a small boat across the bay with a message. Four boat crews were safe and sound in Vågen. They had been farthest south in the Røst Sea when the storm broke, and had not been able to get their sails up in time. They had rowed the whole day, and had only been driven farther and farther away. A cargo ship finally caught sight of them and towed them up to Rookery Island.

But the eighth and last crew had not made it. Johan had the news. They had seen Iver Ellingsa and his sons hoist sail, and they had seen the boat overturned an instant later. Martines Torstensa lay closest. He and his crew managed to row up to the capsized boat. But only one man remained by the time they got there. He was the weakest man in the whole crew, but he had managed to work his way up to the overturned boat and was hanging on for dear life when they got a hold on him and pulled him into the boat.

Two women were widowed, and six children made fatherless along House Brook Road. It had been Ena, Iver Ellingsa's wife, who had been led along the shore when Magda came from the barn. She lost her husband and two sons on the same day. There were no more men in her house.

And a stone's throw or two south in the Homestead, in that gray and unpainted house along the shore, Anna went to bed grieving. Now she knew what the thunderous warning in the loft had been the evening before. The storm had taken two men from her house. The hired man from Borge – and Oluf. She was twenty-five years old, and a widow, and now had complete responsibility for four small children.

There was no burial. There was no one to bury.

The Captain

They came to recognize her by the way she walked. 'Magda walks so beautifully,' they said. It didn't really seem as if she were carrying anything at all when she came north through the Homestead with her water pails. And furthermore, she always dressed so nicely. No one understood how she managed that. She was neither richer nor poorer than most of the people in the Homestead, and she had a house and children and animals to take care of, as the others did who lived along House Brook Road.

Still, in some way, she was different from the others. She was a newcomer, after all. But they were curious about her for more than that. It was difficult to become close to her, the stately young wife from Tuv. It was not easy to know who she really was.

She did not run from door to door, visiting neighbors. But she did come when she was invited. There was only one house she went to without first being invited. That was at Gerda's, right across the road, the wife of Johan Olsa.

When the neighbors visited her, they found her like other people. She pulled out a chair and offered coffee and said,

'Please, have some!' And if there was something going on in the Homestead, she said, 'Oh, don't get too excited, now.'

When there was gossip about the neighbors, she became quiet and stared off into space. 'Well,' she said after a while, 'people are all so different.' And she would suddenly swing around on her stool, dance off laughing to the stove, bring the coffeepot back, pour a cup with her hand on their shoulders, and say again: 'You must have another cup!'

People learned that if they wanted to talk about such things, it was better to go to some other house.

They said about her that she had come from a hard place and a hard father to another hard place and another hard man. He *was* a hard man, Johan, but not toward Magda. From the very first, they had gotten along well together.

Sometimes he drank a little too much at Christmas, and during other holidays. Magda didn't like that. She had a rule: she never danced with anyone who had been drinking. She never said anything to him. But she could tell that he knew she did not like it.

It was as a worker that Johan was hard. He was only of medium height, and rather slight-looking but, whether on land or sea, when it came to work he was a brute. He wanted everything to be done all at once, and he had no use for anyone who could not keep the same pace.

If they were confined to land by bad weather, he paced up and down outside the window all day. And if there were too many days ashore, they could hear him down in the woodshed. Sometimes he just stood there chopping at the empty block.

Before he was twenty, he had been the skipper of his father's five-man boat. Edvard would rather fish with the old fellows in the small boats around Vågen. It was not difficult for Johan to get a good crew. 'That Johan is a winner at sea,' they said.

He was always among the first to the boathouse in the morning. Before the men had finished drinking coffee in the other kitchens, he and his crew had the five-man boat in from the mooring and had the gear on board.

He wanted to be the first one at sea. By the time the old fellow at the north end of the Homestead had hoisted the signal flag, they had usually already shoved off. Then, bending their backs to the oars, they rowed down the bay, and out by Må Point, hoisted the sail.

Johan did not like storms any more than anyone else, but it was still the case that he thrived with a couple of reefs in the sail. It was then that he showed his best.

His boat could be recognized by the fact that four of the men wore sou'westers and one a hat. He always wore a hat at sea. He had a broad-brimmed felt hat he had gotten from his father. So long as he was on board, that hat sat straight on his head. The minute they pulled into port, he pulled it down at an angle over one ear.

★★★

It was several months after the day of the disaster. It was May. The Lofoten season was over, the five-man, eight-oared boats were hauled up on land, and the small boats had been gotten down from the boathouse lofts. The women sat in their kitchens plucking feathers, well into the birding season.

A Mostad winter had passed, a winter that had left its traces behind it. The people were so few, they lived so close to each other, and most of them were related. Hard luck in one house was hard luck for everyone.

Magda was in the kitchen one evening, preparing the baptismal clothes for the twins. Johan had taken a young fellow from south in the Homestead with him and had sailed across the bay in the three-man boat. There had been a book salesman in Mostad who had sold books of home sermons. He had asked Johan to ferry him to the next place.

All at once there was a young girl standing in the doorway. She had been with the pastor all day, studying for confirmation, and, hiking this way, had come with a message for Magda. Johan's boat had capsized outside the Kvalnes headland.

There was not much more to be learned from her. In the middle of the next morning, Johan himself came hiking over the mountain.

The current took them as they rounded the headland and were about to head for Vågen. There had been a strong current, although there was not much wind to speak of. Before they knew what had happened, they were in the water.

They had managed to clamber up on the overturned hull, but the sea began to spin the boat around. As soon as they had hauled themselves up to the keel, they were thrown into the sea again.

The book salesman couldn't swim. The other two had grabbed him by the collar and hauled him with them each time they tried to climb up on the hull again. But finally it became too much for the stranger. When help came, he lay dead across the keel.

Johan began to build the coffin as soon as he got home. The next night he borrowed a boat and took it across the bay. That is how the book salesman began his final trip. To Bodø, on the local boat.

Two Brothers

It was rowing the small boats in the fall that was worst. They usually lay at the Outer Bank, down in Røst Sea. That was where the fishing grounds were. But it was also there that the bad weather came first and hardest. If a storm came up, there was nothing to do but look for one of the little winding channels through which one could find land. A shelter in the shoals, or a narrow little sound in the lee of a small island – those could save both life and boat.

The Må Point channel was such a place. It ran along Må Point, the southernmost and outermost end of the mountain ridge that stretched out along Mostad Homestead.

As a channel it was not much. The fishermen from Vågen called it a miserable channel, and for strangers it was no channel at all. But for the fishermen at Mostad, it was both their point of departure and point of return.

When they came rowing home, nearing Mostad mountain, and had Må Point to port, they slipped in behind a dark and slick little island. That was how you got into the Må channel. After that it ran along a steep mountain wall eastward a couple hundred yards, until they had rounded the point into the bay.

The crucial place was the rock out at the head of the point. In good weather it looked as if they had the whole ocean before them when they rounded the point. But it did not have to be a full-blown southwester before it began to boil up white over a reef just offshore. There was just barely enough room between the reef and the headland for a boat and the oars. The men always had to pull harder at the oars when they slipped through that little sound. Even when the weather was clear, there were almost always a current and strong eddies there. Day and night, year round, the sea lay there gnawing at the smooth-planed flat rock that cut across at an angle down in the deep. One never knew. At any moment a breaker that seemed to come right from the bottom might heave itself up.

The men at Mostad saved some time rowing through Må Channel. They did not have to row outside the shallow ground and the buoy before they eased off. After a long day at sea, it was tempting to try the shortcut, even when the weather was bad. Especially in gale weather they were apt to attempt that treacherous channel. If they made it past the reef, they got home all the sooner.

★★★

Scarcely a year and a half had passed since the accident with the book salesman when disaster hit the Homestead again. And it happened in Må Channel. It was December. Johan had been on the Outer Bank with his handgear to get fish for the Christmas holidays. He had come home, and was sitting at the dinner table.

Magda noticed that he constantly peered out through the window. "I wonder what has happened to Bernt and Johan?" he said after a while. The two boys were brothers, and had been out with their handgear, as he had. They had been right behind him as he rounded Må Point and cut across the bay. The last he had seen of them was when they turned to slip in past the black reef and into the channel.

He left to get someone to go with him. Then he saw that they had already gathered at the landing. They were launching a boat. The boys' father sat in the stern as they set out from land.

It was not long before they came rowing in again. Johan went down to the shore to hear the news. But it was the father they came in with. They had not seen any boat south in the bay. It was then they realized there must have been an accident. And the boy's father could not deal with that. They brought him in.

Still more people came to the beach. They got a bigger boat and launched it. The wind was not bad, but the sea was heavy. It had not died down since the last storm.

It was dark before they came back to land. There were people standing along the rough stone walls on both sides as the boat glided into the landing. Two men sat on the middle seat with a bundle between them.

They had found the capsized boat in Må Channel. It was filled with water, and lay and ground itself against the rock at the head of the point. The mast was driven crookedly through the bottom of the boat. The boat had overturned and driven the top of the mast into the sea floor. The sail and the lines hung and slapped against the hull. One of the boys hung lifeless over one of the seats, his head over the railing, dipping into the sea. His brother was gone.

They pulled the boy into the five-man boat and tore off his upper clothes. They saw he was still warm, and laid him over a seat and began to work on him.

They were still working on him as the boat came out of the

December darkness and into the landing. The boy's father sat bareheaded on a stone down by the shore.

They carried the boy between them up to his mother's kitchen. There they laid him on the oilcloth-covered table, under the kerosene lamp. When they saw him in the light, they knew it was over. It was too late. The sea had taken him as well as his brother.

His mother went to the cupboard under the bench and found a clean hand towel. She unfolded it and laid it over her son's face. Then she took his wet boots and put them in the corner by the stove, as he used to do himself when he came home from the sea.

The Whole Community at Work

But life went on in the Homestead. The men went fishing, as before, and the women tramped up and down House Brook Road with their water pails.

However dark things seemed one year, with storms and shipwrecks and no fish, it seemed to be forgotten the next. And when spring came, the burdens slipped from the shoulders of the people in Mostad, however the winter had gone.

As soon as the fishing in the Lofotens was done, they turned their backs to the sea and became a mountain people. For several busy spring and summer months one continually saw people on the trails up into the mountains.

They always took their dogs with them on the first spring trips up into the mountains. Some took two or three. It was meat they were looking for on those first days in May. There were puffins on the hills and in the rocky slopes on the other side of the mountain. That was magnificent food in the lean months of spring! Genuine holiday fare, as they said. After a long winter with one fish dinner after another, there was no shortage of people who took a trip up into the mountains looking for a little fresh fowl to get their teeth into. Both the men and the women went. Late into the night, young people hiked up in groups, and came down again in the morning with heavy loads.

It wasn't easy to get up to the food pantry on the outer side. Along the whole length of the Homestead, the mountain was so steep that it was impossible for people to climb. But a little south, the broad back of the mountain narrowed, and became a somewhat lower neck before it again lifted its shoulders in exultation and became a mighty cliff, farther out. From the little neck and downward, the mountain eased enough for both heather and grass to put down roots. Halfway down, a ridge pushed out at an angle to the mountain and ran like a gigantic stairway toward the Homestead.

The trail ran along that ridge. At the bottom, it looped around in small arcs, winding its way up between stony ridges and knolls. Then it ran a few yards along the outer side of the hill, toward the Homestead, and disappeared behind a rock or a mound to the other side. It was like climbing a circular staircase. About three hundred feet up, the little ridge developed a hunchback. It was just flat enough for a gate and a few feet of fence on each side. That was to keep the sheep, up there for summer pasture, from coming down into the Homestead. It was there they used to stop for their first rest.

They needed it. From there on, the path cut at a precipitous angle up along the edge of a cliff that ended in Mostad Homestead a thousand feet below. The trail was not much more than a sheep's path up there. It was so narrow that they had to go in single file. There were generally patches of ice on the trail well into spring. They called it the Icy Strait. When they went for puffins in the early spring, they had to take axes to chop footholds in the ice. Icy Strait was the most dangerous part of the path. It occasionally claimed human lives.

Once they had passed Icy Strait, it was safe. Then they were on the mountain itself. The path slipped up over a long and gradual incline. They called that the Snow Meadow because of the way winter lingered so long there.

When they had gone far enough to be able to see over the neck of the ridge toward Outer Bank, they felt as if they had arrived. Although there were still some steep ascents ahead, before they were on top. After the ascent, and before they climbed the last few yards, they usually stopped and caught their breath. Røst Sea lay beneath them and, down there, like a broad sinister band around the edge of the land, the treacherous reef! Green patches in a blue sea, and white foaming breakers in the green.

And beyond everything lay the Røst islands, tossed into the sea. Stavøya like a tail fin sticking up in the air. Wood Island and Big Mountain welded together like the back of a large whale. And farthest out, Nykene, like three mice teeth up out of nothing.

★★★

It was not very far along the ridge to the top. But the trail was windy! Part of it ran along a shelf of land on the side toward Røst Sea, part of it on the hillside toward the cliff overhanging Mostad

Homestead. Finally, it cut steeply up toward an earthen bluff. When they had hauled themselves up over the edge of that, they stood on a broad mountain plateau. It was as flat as a living-room floor and as big as two soccer fields. Grass grew thick and soft over the whole area. A piece of lush lowland up under the clouds where the sheep of Mostad could have their sky-high pasture. The children of Mostad always thought it was a kind of fairy tale the first time they stuck their heads up over the bluff and saw the huge, grass-covered plateau – Broad Mountain – stretched out before them.

But they learned early that if the fog came in while they were up there, they had to use their heads. There was only one place where they could get back down again. On the east it dropped off vertically to the abyss that was Mostad Homestead. Toward the west it went straight into Røst Sea. In good weather one could lie on the edge of the cliff and see the white of the breakers a quarter of a mile below. There was always a white stripe along the shore on the outer side. Not even when the wind was calm did Røst Sea lie completely at peace.

To get to the slope where the puffins nested, they had to cross Broad Mountain. A little path ran across it. Where it ended, the little plateau dropped off onto a steep ridge. It was out there they liked to stand and look around. It was like being on the peak of the roof of the world, they thought. Without having even to shift their feet, they had an open view in every direction. Here lay Rookery Island beneath them with bays and peaks and headlands. It was all small and strange from that great height. Up in the north lay huge Mosken itself looking so insignificant. The sharp peaks of the Lofoten peninsula – they weren't so impressive anymore, either.

But surrounding everything lay the sea, even larger, even more endless than ever.

But it was the puffin slope they came for, early in May, and not the view. It lay to the west, below the plateau. Overhead the birds circled in continual circuits. Northward, along the slope, a swing out over the sea, a dive in toward the land, another flight along the slope, and then out again. A narrow, black, beating wing against a white breast. A whole flapping army in white tie and tails. They weren't great flyers, these puffins, but more persistently than most, they pressed themselves forward through the air with their big, triangular, red and yellow beaks.

The climbers were scarcely down from the ridge before their small yellow dogs were running loose toward the slope, disappearing among the huge, dark gray blocks of stone.

Out by a large flat declivity on the outside edge of the slope, the owner of the dog stopped and prepared to receive the crop. The owner of a proficient dog could have a load of twenty birds when he went back down the trail to the Homestead again. A belt of black and white and yellow-red all the way around his waist.

The people of Mostad caught up to fifteen thousand birds a year, and most of them were puffins. For that reason, puffin dogs were worth their weight in gold. There had been times when a good dog cost as much as a good cow, some of the old folks said.

Scarcely had they begun to carry down the first loads of birds for food from the puffin slopes before it was time to drive the sheep up to the mountains. It was generally about the middle of May that it happened, after the lambing was over.

About the same time, they began to gather eggs. And that was both serious work and fun for the people of Mostad. Long before they were old enough to go along and gather eggs, the little boys went on their own egg-hunting expeditions down in the Homestead. They collected broken shells after their meals and placed them on the rocks and in the crevices of the cliff a few yards above the hillside. They went down to the boathouses and found some rope and coiled it over their shoulders. Then they went hunting for eggs, just like the grown-ups.

They had to be fifteen before they could go up into the big mountains and collect eggs. But already, as thirteen- and fourteen-year-olds, the most adventurous of them began to sneak away. They went to bed like everyone else in the house, and were as quiet as mice until everyone was asleep. Then they sneaked in their stockinged feet down the stairs and out. By the time morning came, it was too late to stop them. They had already returned with their loads of eggs. The competition was intense. It was a matter of who could find the most. The most eager of them went even if it was storming or raining. Usually they went in pairs, and used a rope. But it happened that they sneaked away all alone and hung by their fingers out over the mountain, just to take the lead in the egg-hunting competition.

Sometimes the adults engaged in a little egg-gathering competition, too. But most of them went to find food. Johan Nicholaisa and Oluf Berntsa did it for the sake of both food and sport. They were rowing sidekicks, Oluf and Johan. Oluf was ten years older, but they were always together, one as quick as the other, both at sea and on shore.

Johan was slim, standing as straight as Magda; Oluf broad and bowlegged and rather short. When he walked, he rolled from side to side like an old skipper. He had always done so.

"There is nothing here, and nothing there, and from nothing God created the world," he used to say when they were out fishing with handlines and getting nothing. Oluf was an optimist.

The eyes beneath that bristly mop of light hair were blue and inquisitive. Right in the middle of his face he had a nose as crooked as an eagle's beak. But he followed that nose to good fishing spots and to even better bargains at Petter's store. He could neither read nor write, and he was not beyond superstition. Once he had seen a headless man on the path out by the point.

Most of the time he chattered and laughed, but when he did not get what he wanted, he sulked like a child with a hanging lip. But the moment anyone in the Homestead needed help, he was the first to show up and offer a hand. "That Oluf," people said, "he is at least five different people."

It was kittiwake eggs they went after first in the spring. Kittiwakes laid their eggs on the grassy hillsides down by the sea. They were usually in difficult places, and easiest to reach from boats. One man steadied the boat just offshore while the other clambered up and down among the rocks and brought bags of eggs down to the boat.

Kittiwake eggs were a delicacy for everyone in Mostad, young and old. They never cooked less than a potful. From year to year the children tried to break the household records for the number of eggs eaten. What the women did not boil, they made pancakes of, or else gave them away to those who were not able to get up into the mountains.

In June it was time for auk and guillemot eggs. Auks and guillemots laid their eggs high up in the bluffs on the side of the mountain, so they had to be taken from above. All through June, Johan and Oluf made their regular way up and down the trails with seventy fathoms of rope coiled over their shoulders and light wooden baskets on their backs. They preferred to start out early in the morning and did not return until late in the evening. There were not many in Mostad who were as eager as they were. Both of them climbed like goats.

When they had packed up past Staupan and Icy Strait and Snow Meadow and had come up to the place where the eggs were, Oluf braced himself and dug his heels into the hillside. Then he got a good grip on the line with his short, round fingers. He was the heavier of the two, and the safer one to serve as an anchor.

So Johan let himself down out over the edge of the cliff and disappeared and went as far as the line would let him go. Partly he hung on the rope, partly he clung to small crevices and ledges as he emptied nest after nest. Six hundred feet beneath him, the breakers gnawed at the stone. He lived in the hope that Oluf would not doze off at his post.

But Oluf hung on all day, and slacked off and hauled in as was needed. Every once in a while Johan stuck his head up over the edge and emptied the canvas bag he had around his waist. Then he disappeared into the deep again.

Sometimes the line became suspiciously light, down at the other end. Then Oluf knew that Johan had found a little shelf and was taking a break for a smoke. Or it could mean that he had unfastened himself and crawled out on his own down there, on the side of the mountain, in order to get to a nest he could not reach from the rope.

When they came down the trail late at night, Oluf grinned his broadest grin, whether they had a few or a lot of eggs in the basket: "There now," the optimist said, "that was not a bad day's work!"

Everybody in Mostad worked in the birding season in spring. Throughout May even the oldest fellows went out for their turn. If they were too stiff and slow to walk up into the mountains, they could always hobble down to the boat landing and row out to catch auks and guillemots for autumn's food.

They caught them at sea, right outside the tide line, illegally. They stretched netting between planks and let the birds get tangled in the mesh when they came gliding in to rest on the water. When their underground telegraph was not working as well as it usually did, and the sheriff came unexpectedly, they paid their fines – and went right back to netting birds. It was a matter of storing some food away. Every house needed a couple of barrels of salted fowl if they were going to manage through the fall, when fishing was poor.

The women sat in the kitchens all along House Brook Road. Taking care of the catch was women's work.

Magda was not very good at the business of preparing birds. They never used sea birds for food where she came from. She was always glad to see summer come, but dreaded spring. In her opinion, May was the darkest month of the year. She had enough to do, with the children and the old folks, doing housekeeping and taking care of the animals; she didn't need to sit up all night pulling the gizzards out of birds, too!

But she had promised herself, when she found that birds were a part of living in Mostad, that she would learn how. "Before I finally give up, I am going to master it," she told herself as spring neared and she had to get at it again.

The auks and the kittiwakes were the worst to work with. You had to be as strong as a man to pluck them. The feathers stuck so tightly that they had to be pulled out one by one. When that had been done, they had to be cut open with a sharp knife, all the intestines taken out, and they had to be washed clean.

Day after day, all through May, they carried sacks of birds up to Magda. As soon as she was through with the housework and the outside work for the day, she had to sit down in the kitchen with a sackcloth apron and her wooden shoes. She no sooner finished with one load than they came from the boat landing and tossed a new, dripping wet pile on the floor in the shed. The rest was for her to do. She tied the birds together in pairs and hung them up to dry. As soon as they had dried in the breeze along the south wall, she had to carry them into the house and sit down again. It took up to three hundred birds to make a barrelful.

And then there was a great heap of feathers up in the loft. They sold some, but most of them went into their own bedding. At night, the people of Mostad lived upper-class lives. At Magda's house, not only the pillows and the comforters, but the mattresses, too, were filled with the finest down.

 From the Dawn of Time

They were a mountain people most of all in late summer. Whole families went into the mountains to do the haying. It took a lot of hard-working hands to get enough to feed the cows and sheep all winter. Only those who could not manage the climb up into the mountains stayed home at the Homestead. They were the very oldest and the very youngest.

The field behind the school was the summer pasture for the cattle, so they had to go up into the mountains to find winter feed. There were a few places on the outer side of the mountain where the terrain was not quite so steep. Here and there it leveled out just enough so that a bit of sweet and struggling Lofoten grass could grow. It was on these grassy mountainsides over toward Røst Sea that they did the haying.

When the weather was good, caravans of people crawled up the trail with scythes and rakes over their shoulders, and with water pails in their hands.

The hay fields were divided into twelve parts, and each landowner had his parcel. In addition, there were a few outlying spots open to anyone who did not own anything else.

Those who owned land formed partnerships, and divided the crop equally. It was more practical that way. In the places where it was too steep, one of them could hold onto the line while the other one used the scythe. The women and the children raked the hay into windrows, and turned them in the sun. It was too rugged to set up hay-drying racks. They had to dry the hay on the ground.

The hay was transported by sea. Their hay wagons were boats. They trampled the dry hay into laced-up sacks, and started them rolling downhill toward the beach. If the hillside was really steep, they arranged themselves in stages on the way down. The one on top let the ball of hay go, the next one stopped it a few yards farther down and sent it on to the next one down, and so on. The idea was to slow them down so that they would not roll right into the ocean. When the sack was large and the child was small, sometimes both of them went head over heels downhill.

As soon as there was enough hay for a boatload, they brought a five-man boat around the mountain and began to load the hay on board. And that was not always easy in the restless sea on the outer side.

Petter the shopkeeper had his own method of getting his hay home. He wrapped a line around a big rock and threw it into the water a few yards out. In that way, he kept the boat headed straight into the shoreline while he sat in the bow and hung on to the end of the line. Every time a heavy sea came that tried to toss the boat up onto land, he hauled it safely out from shore. He sat there the whole time until the men up on the mountain had lowered all the hay sacks down into the boat.

Then there was nothing to do except row along the coastline until they had rounded Må Point. They bore in toward Må Point Channel, rounded the headland, and rowed into Mostad bay. Then it was straight in along the shore.

The children loved to watch when the loads of hay came into the Homestead. It was as if a mountain of hay came sailing in. Only the oars, sticking out along the sides, revealed that there were people on board.

No one ever knew when the haying season would end. Such decisions were up to the gods of weather, and they were not always in good humor. The haying season might end in August in the sun and heat, or it might last until October and snow and breakers, when they got the last few straws home.

Sometimes, when they had cut the whole patch and dried it, a torrent of wind would sweep away everything in the course of a night. Then there was nothing to do but look for another patch, and begin all over again. Go where it was so barren and steep that no one wanted a portion of it.

When there was no more hay to be found on the outer side, they had to clamber around the mountain on the inner side. On that black wall of the mountain that hung over the Homestead, there were a few shelves of land a few yards wide. The sea birds had fertilized them since the dawn of time. There the grass grew. If they used lines, they could get up there with scythes. It was possible to find a sack of hay here and there. One only had to kick them over, and they got where they were supposed to be.

Nothing got in the way of a Mostader when he was hunting for hay. If he were going to remain in Mostad, it was necessary for him to keep his cows and his sheep alive throughout the winter. And for that reason, he took his scythe and cut everything he could find in every little mountain shelf above every vertical drop; for that reason he harvested every blade in every avalanche-ready, rocky slope and every hillside down by the foaming sea.

And in spite of that, there was never enough. In the lean grip of spring, the women had to cook fish heads for the cows, and go down to the beach and gather kelp. And the men climbed the mountain as early as spring would allow and pulled small tufts of grass from the small, south-facing crevices as soon as the spring sun managed to force out something green.

Twilight Time

The sea birds were both the first and the last act of summer in Mostad. It ended in August up in the field north of the school, when the auks squawked 'Goodbye!' and 'Thank you!' and plowed their way south.

On August evenings, the people in Mostad hiked up to the field in a body. On really nice evenings it was a virtual emigration as it began to get dark. They went to see all the auk fledglings as they left their childhood homes up on the side of the mountain and fluttered out toward their mothers, calling from water's edge.

Those straggly little clumps of feathers came roaring down as if they had been thrown into the air, flailing and floundering with their stumpy little wings, trying to reach the sea. But not all of them succeeded in their baptism of fire. Wham! and they bellyflopped on the grassy field, and had to hike the rest of the way to the shore.

As soon as one of the youngsters had tumbled to the ground, and began to chirp his way through the clumps of grass toward the beach, both large and small Mostaders were on the spot. It was fun to look for the young birds, pick them up, and carry them out toward the shore, saving them from a humiliating hike.

Magda did not go up to the field on nights like that. She did not like to go up to the field with dogs and kids and everyone else just to hear birds squawk in the dark. She sat in her kitchen on those autumn evenings, spinning wool, weaving and sewing.

Magda's kitchen was light blue, and large, and had windows facing north and south. She had curtains with embroidered flowers on the valances and on the decorative banding below.

The table stood in front of the south window. That was their headquarters. Whether it was mealtime or not, they sat there, children and grown-ups alike.

Magda made the clothes for everyone in the house, from top to bottom. Everything from underwear to a suit for church had been sewn by her. Even while they slept, Magda had her hands around them. There was not much linen in the house that she had not woven.

Maren, grown old, had knit a bit those first few years, but the arthritis soon became so bad that she had to give up. Then that became Magda's work, too. She sat with her handwork throughout the evening until she was alone in the kitchen. Most of the time, she was the one who blew out the lamp.

It was especially the thick outer socks that took time. Their winter footwear. First you had to knit the socks from thick yarn, and then sew old mittens on for extra soles. Each of them had to have two or three pairs if they were to have something dry to put on. If you were going to hike out into the snow, whether up to the church at Christmas time or down to the shore, you had to have outer socks. Yes, and when spring came, whether they were out after birds or eggs or going up to hay, they used overstockings then, too.

During the dark days of autumn, the men lived indoors, too. That was a busy time in Mostad. They had barely gotten the sheep down from the mountain pasture and done the slaughtering before they sat down to get ready for winter and the Lofoten fishing. Johan had to prepare for his crew. He sat in the kitchen just as Magda did. Sat and sharpened hooks and overhauled the longline gear. Everything happened at the kitchen table, under the light from the only lamp in the house.

As fishermen do, Mostaders lived in the hope of a big haul. But there was scarcely any time of the year when they needed hope more than they did in the fall. Autumn was a lean time of the year. Money was never in such short supply in the Homestead as it was then.

It was not often that it was possible to row out with the handgear and the small boats. And when the weather was good enough so that they could get out to sea, there were usually only a few small cod to be had. Petter bought whatever they had to sell and hung it up along the store wall, but even so, for most of them it was a time of debt. The closer they were to Christmas, the poorer they became. So they had to go and ask for credit. Petter said Sure, and let them have what they needed.

But the people in Mostad took pride in their honesty and credit. A debt was something they were not supposed to have. As a consequence, they pushed themselves and their boats all the harder, and rowed out on days when they should have stayed at home. At home, their wives made the rounds, and were afraid.

When the men were on their way home on autumn evenings, they used to gather outside the mountain and row together through Må Point Channel and up the bay. It was safer that way, should anything happen.

If the wind was astern when they came to the bay, they hoisted their sails and came in like a flock of black birds in a storm, along the shadowed coastline. After they had reached land with their little catch, they lighted lanterns and hung them up on the boathouse walls. All along the shoreline, the lights blinked side by side as they stood there and cleaned the fish. Fifteen or twenty figures in pairs; pairs in the cones of light.

And when Petter saw that they were out to sea, and paying a little against their debts, he was happy and praised them and gave them more goods. In that way they managed to get from day to day, more or less. With their pride intact, and in eternal debt nonetheless.

But when Saturday night came, peace settled over the neighborhood of Mostad, whatever the weather or the fishing or the debt at Petter's.

When the darkness began to settle in over the roofs of the houses, and it was still too early to light the lamps, they settled into twilight in their kitchens. The children sat in a clump in front of the stove, opened the firebox door, and had both a fireplace and a television screen. They warmed themselves in the red glow and saw wonderful things in the coals, while the grown-ups chatted among themselves, or told about the times when they had been children. Sometimes Magda took the guitar down from the bedroom wall and sang some of the songs she had learned from her mother at home, in Tuv.

Martines

Beneath the north window in Magda's painted blue kitchen, there was a narrow wooden bench covered with woven rugs. It was there that they hunched up to sit, those who dropped by. There were enough of them. But some came more often than others. The one who came most often was Martines Torstensa, Johan's uncle.

Martines was in his fifties, and a big, sturdy fellow. A heavy black beard hung down over his chest. What could be seen of his face was broad and clean-cut and ruddy. Up around his ears, his black beard became curly brown hair. But in the middle of all that red and black and brown, things blinked gently blue.

Martines chose not to get involved in people's quarrels. If he had his own opinions about what was going on here or there in the Homestead, he kept it to himself. He was dependable and good-natured and never boasted about himself, but when he came by he always had something interesting to talk about. About the only flaw in his life was how much he loved coffee. And being as unobtrusive and cautious as he was, he found it impossible to get right to the point when he stopped by and was thirsty.

There was always coffee for him at Magda's anyway. She liked Martines, so as soon as he showed up at the door, she went over and put on the coffeepot. 'Oh, Magda, don't make a fuss over me,' he said, 'You need the little you have!' as he sat down to wait for the coffee. And when he had satisfied the worst of his thirst for coffee, and was about to go, he beamed like the sun. 'Well, bless you, Magda!' he said.

The last they always saw of him was his homespun backside and his sheath knife. Martines was so big that he bent double to go through the door.

It was a housewife's holiday for him to be invited to the neighbors for dinner. He was a widower, and had been one for a long time. He had not been married for many years before tuberculosis took Andrea, his wife. She had, though, given birth to three sons. They were Alfred, Frithjof, and Thorvald. They were not even of confirmation age when their mother died. Martines took over as best he could. In the winter, when he was out rowing for Lofoten fish, he hired a girl to do the housekeeping; otherwise he managed things by himself.

Martines had already been tested. He had lost someone even before Andrea. Petra was her name, and she had been scarcely eighteen years old. They were engaged, and were going to be married when summer came. They had even planned what kind of food to have at the wedding. They had been together up in the mountains, one May night, together with a number of other young people, to catch puffins.

About three in the morning, they were on their way back down the mountain with their catch. There was laughter and life and joking, and nothing but bright, clear weather. Martines was right in the middle of the column as it wound down the trail, with Petra close behind him.

In Icy Strait, Petra turned to ask the girl directly behind her for some of the words to a song they had been singing. Before she got an answer, she had stepped off the edge of the path, and fallen. They saw her for the first few yards. She clawed with her fingers at the grassy slope. She almost came to a stop at a clump by the cliff, but the grass was slippery in the morning dew, her speed too fast, and the weight of the puffins too heavy.

The last Martines saw was the tuft of moss in her hands. He found her among the stone rubble a thousand feet below, at the foot of the mountain. She lay in a wreath of puffins.

Martines came to Johan's father that morning, woke him, and asked him to help carry her down. So Martines went to the cemetery instead of to the altar. The wedding feast became a wake. The pastor wrote in the church records: 'Petra Ulriksen, fell from the precipice. Found crushed at the foot of the mountain.'

There was another young girl with them that night. That was Andrea. After several years, they were married, and lived well and happily. Until sickness took her from him. For the second time, he went to the cemetery in Nordland with someone he loved.

But he had sons. They grew up to be strapping, hard-working, decent fellows.

And then disaster came to the Homestead again. It was not many years after Magda had moved to Mostad. Martines's oldest son was twenty-eight, the youngest eighteen.

It was just before Christmas. Suddenly one day, the middle one became sick. No one knew what was wrong, but he became worse and worse. After several days, they carried him down to a boat, rowed across the bay, and put him on the local boat to Bodø. He was dead in his bed the first morning he was in the hospital. Some kind of kidney disease had killed him.

In Martines's house, they had to get everything ready. Martines himself went around and invited everyone to the funeral. When anyone tried to comfort him, he answered: 'It was meant to be. That's all. It was meant to be.'

Christmas and New Year's and January came. Magda had just finished preparing breakfast one morning, and stood looking out through the window into the morning darkness. She saw someone come rowing along the shore towing an empty boat. She tossed some heavy clothes on and ran down to hear what had happened. Some of her men were at sea, too, that day.

Martines sat in the boathouse and wept. The empty boat lay down at the landing. It was his sons' boat.

They had rowed out early to catch a little fresh fish for dinner. Alfred had wakened his youngest brother and talked him into coming along. But they had not gotten any farther than out by the point. The overturned boat was found swamped in Må Point Channel by the boat that had rowed out after they had.

People ran out to the point to look for the boys. By the time they came to the outermost point, Alfred and Thorvald had been driven in toward land and lay there side by side pounding against the rock. The sea held them up. Every time they started to sink, the waves pushed them back up atop the black, slippery rock. It was too dangerous to try to get at them from land. They had to be brought in by boat.

As the boys were carried up from the landing, their father sat on the front steps mumbling their names. Martines had lost everything he had; he was finished and broken. The only one who remained was the housekeeper who worked for him. She stood behind him in the entryway, listening to him moan. 'Martines,' she said, 'I will stay with you. I will always be here.' 'What will we two do?' sighed Martines without looking up.

Just up from the boathouse there was a yellow-painted drying shed owned by Karine. It was where they laid those who had died at sea or up in the mountains. The tiny sod-roofed shed was a chapel for the people of Mostad. When children had to walk along the shore, and it was dark, they always hurried by. Alfred and Thorvald were carried up there. Magda came with a basin of water and a cloth and took care of the boys. No one had asked her to: she just came.

Martines went from door to door to invite people to the funeral. It was the second time within six weeks. Well into the night, there were hammer blows from Edvard Nicholaisa's carpentry shop. Standing there in the light of a lamp, he built coffins. First one, and then another.

On the day of the funeral they stood in black, side by side in Martines's white-washed, paneled kitchen. The house was filled with people, clear out onto the entryway. Those who wanted to said goodbye to the boys, and then Edvard screwed the lids down.

It was not easy to find anything to decorate the coffins with in the winter, but the two boys each had a wreath of heather. And up out of the heather, a few flowers from Magda's windowsill.

After the Word of God had been read for the procession, Johan began to sing 'Nearer My God to Thee.' He was not a churchgoer, but he had a good strong voice, and usually led the singing at funerals in Mostad.

When they had threaded the caskets out through the entry doors, and begun the procession down to the landing, it was Martines himself who started the singing. He began with 'Behold a Flock.' First he sang alone, and then, gradually, the others joined in. By the time they reached the shore, they were a whole choir.

It was quiet winter weather. The clouds hung low and heavy with snow over the Homestead. On the shore, the sea drove up and ran back between the stones. They rowed across the bay with several boats in the procession. Martines sat in the stern of the first, a casket on each side. He sat and sang hymns all the way across the bay, until the keel ground against the stones at the landing in Sørland.

They threaded oars through the handles on the coffins. The bearers were all boys. Three on each side, six for each casket. Twelve in all. The first person behind the caskets was Martines in his church suit. And after him, half of the Homestead in Mostad; as many as there had been room for in the five-man, eight-oared boats. As they passed each home they stopped, put down the caskets, and sang a hymn.

They proceeded through the village of Sørland, up the rocky path through Skåret. They filed down to the shore on the other side and around the wide Brei inlet, until they reached Nordland Church. By the time they put the caskets down in the snow-white little cemetery by the edge of the sea, they had walked nearly six miles. Out in the mist, Mosken stuck up out of the ocean like a fitting chapel. On the shore below the stone wall, the waves sounded like an organ.

After they had thrown earth upon the caskets, Martines went to the side of the grave. He bent over the edge and said softly: 'The Lord gave and the Lord has taken away. Blessed be the name of the Lord.'

The funeral procession broke up. Four men with shovels stayed behind. Before the pastor had reached the sacristy door, they heard the first dull thumps of the frozen clods of earth as they landed on the lids of the coffins.

The four men did not straighten their backs until the grave was filled. Then they joined the group that waited for them outside the gates. There was not much time. January days were short, and they had to begin the hike back so that they would get to the boats before it became pitch dark.

At the post-funeral gathering, they served porridge, as was the custom. Magda and some of the young girls sat with their guitars and played and sang, careful not to make the songs too sad. The men sat along the walls and did not say anything.

There was only one speech. Martines himself gave that. He stood up and thanked everyone.

It was an evening in September. The fog lay raw and clammy over Mostad. No one went outdoors.

Far south in the Homestead, a hinge squeaked in an entry door. A stout little female figure stepped out onto a doorstep, and latched the door behind her. She pulled her sweater tightly about herself, and went north up between the houses. Every time she passed a lighted window, it shined on her white kerchief. Otherwise, she was as black as the night she walked in.

The farther north she went, the slower her footsteps became. When she had gotten almost as far north as the store, she stopped for a moment before she took the path down to a white-painted house on the shore.

Magda and Johan were about to blow out the lamp and climb up to the loft when they heard the cautious knocking at the door. It was Anna. She shut the door quietly behind her and stood over where visitors sat. Magda asked her to sit, but Anna said she was only going to be a moment and would remain standing. Stood there, looking first at one and then at the other. At Johan, who sat with his longlines, and at Magda.

'Can you take Karluf?' she finally said. She had come to give away her youngest boy. Four years had passed since she was widowed by the shipwreck of the big eight-oared boat in 1910. She had struggled as well as she had been able, to scratch together what she and the children needed. The spinning wheel had hummed without rest. The neighbors had been helpful and brought food to her, but they were limited in what they had. She could not be an eternal burden on them, either.

'What will happen to the poor children?' Those were the last words her husband had wailed from the overturned boat before the breaker took him. The dear Lord had heard him and taken one of the four home to himself: a week after the shipwreck the youngest child died of pneumonia.

The next one had been taken by one of his rowing partners. When Anna came and asked whether he would take the oldest boy, Haftor, he said yes. He was the only one of the five in the boat who had survived. He had not forgotten her husband's last cry. He was about to move to Vesterålen, and took Haftor along to be a goat herder.

But Anna still had two at home. Karluf was just barely of school age. He spent so much time at Magda and Johan's. She thought he would be treated well if he were with them. And for that reason, she had knocked on their door this late night in September.

Johan had to say no. Magda's own family was already big enough, and they did not even have their own house. It was divided with Johan's relatives. And Johan's mother had to be taken care of like a child herself. Arthritis had crippled her. She could not even manage to run a comb through her hair.

Anna said thank you, anyway, and left.

She could not bring herself to plead for Karluf at other places. The next time she put her kerchief on and started walking north, it was for her six-year-old Edith that she went.

A fellow from Mostad had come home on a short trip from America to be married. Now they were getting ready to leave. They said they were willing to take the girl with them.

The light was on late into the evening at Anna's those last evenings before they were to leave. She sat by lamplight mending clothing.

On the day they were to leave, Anna was not to be seen in the Homestead. Not even when they got into the boat to row across the bay. She said goodbye to Edith at home in her kitchen. A neighbor came and took the youngster down to the landing where the boat waited. But when the boat pushed out into the bay, Anna sat by her window and watched. She watched them until they rounded Nupen on the other side, and disappeared.

Magda was in Vågen when it was time for the local boat to leave. It lay out a bit, at anchor. They used a small tender to get on board. Magda went out with the tender. She wanted to meet her sister, who was on board the steamer, on her way to Bodø.

Just as they came alongside the ship the newlywed fellow from Mostad suddenly became ill. They barely got him up the ladder and on board. His wife was frightened. No one knew how serious the attack was. She thought it would be risky to take little Edith on that long journey when things were like that with her husband.

So the girl and her suitcases were loaded back into the small boat. Magda took her back to Mostad. Led her back along the way she had come. Up through Vågen and over to Sørland. There they got a ride back across the bay.

Anna stood in the boathouse when the boat came into the landing. She didn't ask what had happened. She just took Edith by the hand and went south along the shore with her. She did not stop before she got into her house.

Up in the loft, Magda was in charge. She was in control in the little, light green, north bedroom where she and Johan had their bed, and she was in control in the yellow room toward the sea where the children were. They had had four children in her first five years in Mostad.

In the rest of the house, Maren held the power. Had it not been for her arthritis and the steep stairs up to the loft, she would have been in control both upstairs and down. Magda allowed her mother-in-law to hold the power. She was determined not to have a falling-out with Johan's mother. The house was too small for that.

Maren ruled from the chair over by the stove, and she ruled without much talk. But when she did speak, the words carried weight. 'It is good weather now for drying clothes,' she might say. And then Magda would put on her apron and go put the clothes to soak in the tub. With as many people as there were in the house, there were always clothes to wash.

Johan had learned how to work from his mother. Even after he had become the skipper of the boat, and married, he could lie in the loft in the morning and hear his mother's voice through the plank flooring: 'The weather today is just right for tarring the three-man boat!' She said it loud enough so that her son was certain to hear.

Maren was not the type to offer much praise. But when Magda had been out in the winter, wrestling water pails through the snowdrifts, she generally came in to find dry and warm stockings hanging by the stove.

After the first winter, Maren asked her to come over to her in the corner by the stove, and told her: 'You are a really hard worker, you are!'

Then a couple winters went by, and she said something again: 'I have been pretty quick at things in my time, but you are even quicker!'

Edvard was quite a different type from Maren. To be sure, he had been a skipper and kept tight control over his own boat, but before he became sixty he had turned the helm over to Johan, and gone ashore. After that, Edvard lived his life in the carpentry shop behind the house. He made doors and windows for people, or whatever it was they needed, from porridge ladles to coffins.

But when winter came, the old man became restless. Although he had given up his boat, he had not given up the sea. When all the men were at sea and it became too lonesome to continue like any other old fellow at home, he got his things together and left, too. Took his wooden food chest and his bedding roll and rowed over to Vågen and found a place to stay. There were some old men over there who fished for a few weeks each winter season.

Edvard was a religious man. It was he who was asked to read from the Scriptures when they held the Christmas party at the school. At home, there were devotions on both Saturday night and Sunday morning.

He had been pretty wild as a youngster, never saying no to either women or alcohol. It was not until much later, in his adult years, that he changed. Ingolf, one of his sons, had come home one Sunday morning with his fiddle under his arm, after having played for a wedding in Sørland. He came back to the Homestead, seeming to be drunk. But it was not alcohol. As evening came, and they were about to go to bed, he said to his father: 'Aren't you going to have evening devotions?'

It was then that Edvard realized that the boy must have had some kind of unusual experience on his way home, at the edge of the sea. It had never been a regular custom for him to hold evening devotions, and the boy had never asked him to do it, either. Ingolf had been converted that night. It made such an impression on Edvard that before long he became a believer, too.

Having converted both himself and his father, Ingolf packed his bags and emigrated to America. Once there, he became a choir director in Wisconsin.

For Magda, one day in Mostad was just like the next. There was always something to do, from the time she put one foot out of bed onto the loft floor in the morning, until she kicked off her wooden shoes and went to bed at night. She was the first one up and the last one to bed.

Everything had its time and place in Mostad. At eight in the morning there were the morning chores in the barn; at two, midday chores; and at eight again, evening chores. At ten in the evening the windows were dark along House Brook Road. It was night in Mostad.

Sometimes in the winter Magda dreamed that she stood and struggled in the snowdrifts, and never got anywhere with her water buckets. And when she woke, there was nothing to do but heave herself out of bed and start out with her water buckets anyway. No one shoveled the snow from House Brook Road in the winter. It wasn't necessary. The women tramped it down.

And then there was the food to prepare. Johan and the hired crew came down from the loft and had to get ready to row out. And when *they* were out of the house, there were the old folks and the children. And the animals.

But first and last, there was the water to carry. Even when Johan was ashore for a day, it was still women's work to carry water. Magda never asked Johan to do that. He had enough of his own work to do, she thought.

And what *he* did was not all that much fun, either. She was reminded of that from time to time. As if she had not known it before.

Late one autumn, he and his father had been to an auction in Sørland. On their way home, they had to go out around Kvalnes and pick up Edvard's tool chest. He had done a little carpentry in a house out there. The whole trip took so long that it was dark when they finally got into the bay and set course for Mostad.

The wind was from the southeast. Right away, they got a good wind for sailing. The sail was in a taut bow; the boat plowed toward home through the uneasy autumn sea, splitting wave after wave and leaving a wake behind it. Overhead, the clouds ran a race with the boat. They would sail over a dark and blackened sea, and then the clouds would part, leaving a gleaming, moonlit sea; another cloud would come sailing and block out the yellow moon again.

Johan was at the tiller, tending the sail. Edvard had put his oilskins over his tool chest in the forehold, and sat on the middle seat in his homespun sweater and sou'wester. He sat and sang.

He did that when he was out sailing. He usually sang the hymns he had learned when he was young.

The gale hit them in the middle of the fjord as the old man was singing, 'Where God leads me, I am glad.' In the first gust of the storm, the boat tipped over, and they were in the water. There was room on the overturned hull for only one. Johan hauled himself up and lay sprawled over the keel. He lay there and held his father up out of the sea until help came. A passing Mostad boat in their lee had seen them in the light of the moon.

'It was so fine to lie in the sea,' Edvard said the day after he had regained his strength. He had been so exhausted that only Johan's grip had saved him from sinking into the sea.

Johan did not say much about what had happened. But at night he was so restless that Magda had to sit up and hold him.

Widow

Early in the morning, a month after Edvard and Johan had capsized on the bay, Karine and Joakim sat at their breakfast table. The house lay a little up from the yellow drying shed, almost at the road. It was two-storied, and painted white, and had green window trim and gables, as did most of the houses in Mostad.

Joakim was forty-three, and Karine was ten years older. Both of them were short, and Karine rather plump. She had a full head of black hair. People said it was so long that she could sit on it when she let it down. But her face was small and round, and as white as chalk.

New snow had fallen during the night. Just then, they heard a voice outside the window. It sounded like a child's voice: 'Karine,' the voice said, 'tomorrow you are going to die.'

Joakim jumped up and ran out. But there was no one to be seen. There were no tracks in the new snow. 'All right, then,' Karine said, 'if I die, it will be God's will.'

Joakim intended to go to Vågen the next day and work on a fishing sloop he had bought. There were a couple fellows who had planned to go across with him in a three-man boat, but something came up.

'Well, then, I will go alone,' Joakim finally said. Karine prepared a lunch for the green wooden lunchbox he used when he was at sea, and put on the lid. 'All right,' he said. 'All right,' she said. And he went out the hall door in his oilskins.

*

Magda had washed clothes and was hanging them on the drying rack down by the shed. She stood there, watching Joakim as he left. The wind had come up, and he was carrying quite a lot of rocks down into the boat for ballast. As soon as he was done, he went on board, hauled out to the buoy, and began to hoist sail.

But even before he had set the sail, a gale blast tipped the boat so far that the sea filled it. Magda saw no one she could call to. It was quiet in the Homestead. It was just after the midday meal, when the men lay down for a short nap.

She ran down the shore. A couple of young boys were launching a boat. When they got there, it was too late. It had happened in an instant. The boat was so loaded with stone ballast that it sank right to the bottom. Joakim couldn't swim. He hung on to the prow until the sea washed over his head.

Karine stood on the shore when they brought him in. She had seen everything from her kitchen window. They carried him past her up to the house. They tried to assure her that he must be alive, because they had gotten him ashore so soon.

'No,' Karine said. 'Just be quiet. He is dead.'

And it was true. He was dead. She said it so calmly. She was used to having such things happen. She had lost a man to the sea before. She was a widow for the second time.

A day passed, and Anna came and offered to clean the house for the burial. She could not bring Joakim back to Karine. But she had two hands. And she had lost a husband, too, just as Karine had.

The pastor came across the bay. He came and sat for about a half hour. They talked a little. After they sang a few hymn verses, he left. He did not come to Mostad every day. There were other widows in other houses who wanted him to stop by. Those from last year, and those from the year before that.

★★★

'It is a law for us,' Karine said on the day they took Joakim to his grave. She had said the same thing twenty-five years earlier when her first husband died.

His name had been Bernt Leonard. He had had more than his share of hard times before the sea got him. Three times it had been a matter of life and death.

The first time had been on the isthmus, way up the bay, cutting hay. A driving rain blew in from the south and churned up the bay. In the evening, they found the overturned boat. It lay hammering against the rocks on the beach. Karine sat in Mostad, a widow.

But in the morning they came, rowing Bernt Leonard from Sørland. He had dragged himself ashore on the other side of the bay, on the sand beach beneath Håen. From there it was impossible to try to reach Mostad along the land. Håen rose thirteen hundred feet straight up from the sea. Not even sheep could make their way along the shore.

In the snow, he had clawed his way up a steep cleft south of Håen. Up on top, he had found a fissure that led down on the other side. It was not too steep to allow him to slide his way down to Sørland Bay. From there, he had only to follow the shore around until he came to a house in Sørland. There they took care of him, got him dried off and thawed out.

Several winters later, Bernt Leonard shipwrecked again. That was on the Outer Bank, outside of Mostad Mountain, about five o'clock on an October afternoon. A breaker came in over them, and the boat flipped. Karl, his companion, had never learned to swim, and disappeared immediately. Bernt Leonard hauled himself up on the overturned boat.

There was a strong current offshore that carried him out into Røst Sea. It became dark, and before long he could not make out Rookery Island. After driving him out for several hours, the current shifted and carried him up to Rookery Island again. He came to a beach, so near that he could have jumped ashore, but he didn't dare. He couldn't touch bottom, and he was too weak to swim.

He was driven by the current the whole night. He glimpsed houses on Nordland as he went by. He called out as strongly as he could, but he saw no lights on land.

As morning drew near, he had been carried all along the

whole outer side, and was coming east to Long Island. Then the current shifted again, and he was driven out to sea once more, headed for Mosken.

But before he had been driven too far offshore, they heard his calls at a small house down by the shore.

So they came rowing, and picked him up. It was eight in the morning. He had knelt on the hull for fifteen hours, and been driven halfway around Rookery Island. About twelve miles on the open sea. The flesh on his knees and legs was gnawed to the bone.

It was his sheath knife that had saved him. He had driven it into the keel as soon as he had gotten up on the hull, and had hung on to it ever since.

During the day, word was sent to Mostad that he had been found. Karine sat there, mistakenly widowed for the second time. She had a husband with more lives than most men, like a cat.

In the evening, Bernt Leonard came to the Homestead himself. Before he lay down in bed, he went to a dresser drawer and got a little black book with gold letters on the cover. *Christian Calendar*, it said on the outside, and inside it said, Damm & Son.

For October 31 he wrote:

On this day I was rescued after having been adrift at sea a whole autumn night, and reunited with my dear wife at home.

I will long remember the day this accident occurred, and Karl died. I become sad thinking about it.

May God be thanked and praised for his goodwill toward me.
Bernt Leonard

A winter passed, and a summer, and autumn came again. By that time, Bernt Leonard had used up his share of God's goodwill.

No one knew how it happened. They had been on the Outer Bank in a small boat and had not returned when night came. The next morning their boat came drifting in toward land and beached at the north end of the Homestead.

Karine was twenty-four at the time. She was nine months pregnant and had three small children. And the previous winter she and Bernt Leonard had taken in a young girl whose father had been lost at sea. There were even more in the house. Karine took care of Bernt Leonard's mother and father, and her ninety-two-year-old grandmother.

But finances were not as impossible for Karine as they had been for Anna. Bernt Leonard had owned the five-man boat himself, and manned it with hired hands. They were paid a fixed salary, and when the year's catch was good, he could save a few kroner.

He had sold the fish in Bergen himself; had been his own agent, so to speak. He had left a few thousand kroner in the bank. That gave Karine courage. Every winter she hired a crew and housed them, as they had done before, and had them man the boat for her. Every summer she sent dried fish to Bergen with Petter Kristensa.

For sixteen years she carried on like that, and managed to do quite well. Then she hired a man from Salten. That was Joakim. He was neither more attractive nor homelier than most of the hired crew, but there was a wedding. They had a daughter whom they christened Eldore. There was not time for much more.

They had been married only a few years when the sea closed over Joakim outside the Homestead.

Karine had to set to work one more time. But her head of black hair was white before a year had passed.

After Joakim's death, she stayed mostly in the kitchen. There were only she and little Eldore now. There was plenty of room around the kitchen table.

On Sundays she put on her black skirt and white blouse. While dinner was on the stove, she took the devotional book down from the shelf and read. When she closed the book, she bowed her head in thanks.

But before two years had passed, it happened again. Her son-in-law was visiting from Saltdalen. He had come with a cargo of timber on a sloop on his way out, and had his brother along as a crew member.

They wanted to get a little fresh fish to take home with them. They borrowed a boat and intended to go just outside Mostad Mountain a little way. It was a bright day in May. They never returned to land. They never even found an oar.

Over in Salt Valley, Karine's daughter sat with three unprovided-for children. She, like her mother, had become a widow.

For Love of Norway

There was a light yellow poster hanging on the wall in Petter's store. It had a picture of a farmer, with a team of horses hitched to a plow. The land was large and rolling. In the background lay a large farmyard with several buildings and a flagpole and a road lined with poplars. Overhead the sky was bright and blue.

That paradise was framed with a wreath of flowers and green leaves. Above the wreath, in large scroll script, it said: TRAVEL WITH THE NORWEGIAN AMERICA LINE TO CANADA.

There was a balance, though, to the tempting call of the America Line. There was another poster on the wall of Petter's store. It was red, white, and blue. A cardboard flag. Right in the middle of the flag there was the figure of a medallion-draped, uniformed man. King Haakon's coronation picture. FOR LOVE OF NORWAY, it said in heavy dark letters in an arc over his head.

Mostaders lent more weight to the king's word than they did to that of the America Line. Most of them chose to remain on the plain at the foot of the mountain.

But hard luck came often after 1910. In three years, Mostad had lost nine men at sea. It could not be denied that when the men were plucked, one after the other from the houses in the little neighborhood, it affected their thinking. There were not that many to choose from.

When they dropped in on each other, from time to time, they preferred to talk about something else. They knew they had to be at sea if they were to make a living.

But when Martines's boys were lost in the shipwreck in Må Point Channel, that was the third disaster in a row. There were those who began to call it Hard Luck Homestead after that. Sometimes the young boys joked among themselves about whose turn it would be next winter.

A few began to wonder a little whether or not there might be places where it would be both easier and less dangerous to settle down. And furthermore, there was a limit to the number of families that could live on the tiny pasture land beneath Mostad Mountain. The most adventurous of them reasoned that, if they were going to travel at all, they might as well travel a long way.

In 1913 the first to go packed up and left. They had scraped together enough money for their tickets and sailed off for Canada, as it said on the poster. There they settled into salmon fishing and farming and carpentry.

World War I brought a high cost of living and rationing to Mostad. The winter fishing had been good in 1914. Since winter fishing basically determined how well they would live the rest of the year, things looked good for summer and autumn. The outbreak of the war knocked prosperity to ruins. The shelves in Petter's store emptied quickly, and the prices shot sky high.

But other than that, it was in the columns of the *Lofoten Post* that the war was fought. And because there were only a few who had enough money to afford a subscription, there was not much of a Lofoten Newspaper War, either. It was in the price of coffee and sugar and flour that the people in Mostad noticed the war.

It was their own battles people were concerned about. Battles for food and clothing and their debt at Petter's. But the war years claimed lives in Mostad, too. Four men in four years. It was the mountain that was beginning to make its claims.

Reidar was one of them. A seventeen-year-old from south in the Homestead. He was cutting hay with a scythe on a little patch of grass up by Tinden. He was going to go down and get a sack for hay when he lost his footing.

Magda was standing on the porch steps when it happened. She heard a scream from up on the mountainside and saw a figure fall through the air. Reidar's brother came running and called for help. He had been with Reidar on the hay field, had been just below him, and had seen his brother sail over his head.

Johan was home from the sea, and went along to the base of Tinden and carried the boy home. He put him over his shoulder and carried him along House Brook Road and down to Karine's yellow drying shed.

When the world war was over, another group of men from Mostad got ready to travel away. Fishing had been bad in the winter of 1918. The last year of the war had been the darkest year in anyone's memory. There was no shortage of reasons for breaking up. They packed, and moved to Canada. Those who had left earlier took the newcomers in and gave them room and board until they found work. They took traditional family names for themselves, or the names of the places where they had lived, just as the others had done. There were a dozen 'Mostinger' together. A 'Little Mostad' in a world where there were no five-man boats, no three-man boats, no steep icy trails to climb, and no threatening channels to row.

But there were also those who found their way *to* Mostad during those years. One late summer day, a widower came from the church village on Nordland. He had his roll of bedding over his shoulder and a small boy by the hand. The man's name was Ludvik, and his son, Sigfred. Ludvik was in his forties, and about as fat as poor Anna. They had moved in together, and now he had been to Nordland to get the rest of his belongings: that was Sigfred.

They went through the Nordland pasture land. The way to church for the people in Mostad. It was a two-hour walk along the ocean. The path took off by the innermost house of the neighborhood. First it went up over a long stretch of green plateau along the edge of a chalky white beach. The plain ran along the foot of a huge mountain ridge like a border along the ocean. Outside, the sea stretched as far as the eye could see, and in the bright summer weather, that was a long way. The sun was high overhead; the sea lay slapping easily.

Where the flat shore ended, the path cut up through a ravine. From there on, the trail was as narrow as a sheep path, and wild. It made sudden little unruly hairpin turns up the sides of steep hills, sometimes leaving them balanced on the edge of an abyss of tumbled rocks. And then it shot down to the shore and over slippery stone slabs, washed by the sea. Nature herself determined the route. Overhead the mountain blocked them off, and down below lay the sea.

This was a great adventure for a boy who had never taken the path before. He had dropped his father's hand the moment they were out of the pasture. He ran in circles, off behind patches of grass and huge stones. He was either off to the side or ahead up the trail the whole way, but with his father never too far behind.

The farther they went, the stranger things seemed around them. In one place, the path disappeared in between boulders as large as boathouses. Sigfred had never been on such a walk. And then it was not long before they saw smiling level land before them again. One field so soft and fine, with grass growing up to their knees. The sheep stood among the rocky slopes, two by two, and three by three, and pointed their ears at them. And when they had stared long enough, they ran off in all directions, bleating and swinging their tails.

After the sheep pasture land, the trail dropped off into a

world of monstrous, rounded boulders. Their heavy backs leaned against each other as if they were resting. On the outer side, they had skirts of glistening kelp, lying half in the sea, half on the land. A little farther in they were as white as sand. Sigfred had to run over and stroke the boulders. They were so smooth that they were almost soft, even though they were stone.

From the rolling stone beach, the path ran up a little hillside. On top, there were new things to see. An enormous depression in the landscape bored itself down on the outer side. It was so deep that when Sigfred came to the edge and looked down, he stepped back.

But it was wonderful to stand there, also. The depression opened out toward the sea, and the water gushed in and out with the waves. At the bottom, it glistened green and white with stones and sand. The sea was so clear that, had it not been for its surface, which drove up and down against the cliff, one might have thought that there was nothing but dry air in the basin.

The path ran farther, and down to the shore again. To a wonderful little sand beach and an adventure of driftwood. Here there were logs, large and small, and planks and sticks and boards and ship's ribs from old wrecks. And everything was washed white by the sea, and nice to hold in one's hands. Ludvik took a rest and a tobacco break so that Sigfred would have time to himself in the pile of driftwood. And he found things, and found things, and wanted to take everything with him: boxes with wonderfully big letters on them, secret barrels that no one had opened, and gleaming green glass floats.

There were things to see on the ocean, too. Reefs that made the sea rise and bubble with foaming breakers even though it was quiet. And every once in a while, a peak would stick up out of the ocean and create strange shapes and figures. In one place, it looked as if a ship were lying and heaving against the rocks along the beach. But it wasn't. As they came nearer, they saw it was just stones. A rock as big as many houses.

In another place, a head stuck up out of the edge of the sea, several times as tall as a person. Stood and looked out over the ocean, with a crooked nose and a chin so long that it almost stuck down into the sea. But its forehead was low. Grass grew on the top of its head. There were bird droppings down over its temples, tufts of moss in its ears. 'That is a troll,' Ludvik explained. And he added that it would not be long before the trail would be easier. Sigfred did not bother much about that. He had already run up the next climb. But when he had climbed the knoll to the top, he saw that what his father had said was true. On the other side, the land spread itself out and became a plain.

Out on the plain, the path led up over a grassy hill, up toward a big pass. When they got there, they saw a big bay beneath them, and that was Mostad Bay. On one side there was a plain with houses on it. 'Anna lives in the house farthest out,' Ludvik pointed out. Then they tackled the last part of the way.

Anna had managed things for herself during the years of widowhood and the world war with both Edith and Karluf to take care of. She had not been able to get herself to try to give children away a third time.

The eight hundred kroner she had gotten as a one-time pension payment when her husband had gone the way of all flesh had not lasted long. But she had gotten down to work and stretched out the work day. She had carded wool and spun and knitted and cared for the kroner in such a way that she had managed in a fashion. She was terribly careful in everything that she did, and had a regular routine for each day, from the time she got up until she went to bed.

When things were hardest, the others brought food to her. It was the custom in Mostad that they 'brought to' when anyone suffered from hardship. They came with milk and meat and potatoes, and saw to it that there was food on the table.

Anna was the one they 'brought to' most often. She never asked for help, but the others could tell from watching the children when things were bad for them. They were often hungrier than the other children in the Homestead. If they were given a slice of bread in someone's house, they took it with them and went out behind a boathouse and ate it. And made their meal last as long as possible.

But Anna wasn't the easiest person to bring food to. She was always so happy to fix something for people when they came. The people who 'brought to' Anna had to be quick to leave, else it turned into refreshments, and not help.

And then Ludvik came, broad and short and good-natured. With brown eyes and bushy brows and a carefully tended mustache. His wife had died of some illness, and he was as available as Anna.

They met the first time in Skåret between Sørland and Nordland. Anna was struggling up the steep hillside with a heavy cardboard box filled with wool that she had gone to Sørland to get. Ludvik caught up with her in a curve and asked if he could carry the box for her. From that time on it was the two of them. That was in 1917. Anna had been a widow for seven years.

They put together what they had of children and trifles, and there was new life in the southernmost house in the Homestead. Ludvik had not been in Mostad very long before Anna started her second brood.

But poverty was in the house as it had always been. There were no more animals or more land than before. They had to work for others to get whatever they had. Anna sat by the spinning wheel as before, and Ludvik found a job on a boat and went to sea. When there was no fishing, he took whatever odd jobs there were. In the evenings he sat in the basement and carved wooden clogs for sale.

However hard they worked, there was always a shortage of money. No one had to charge things at Petter's as often as they. And no one liked to do it less, either. When there was no one at the store when he came, and it was closed, he waited until someone did come. He thought it was unpleasant to knock at Petter's door and get him to open the store when he had to ask for credit.

He established a waiting room at Magda's. Petter did not keep regular hours. Magda was the nearest neighbor. It was easy to wait at Magda's.

'Hu, hu, hu,' he said when he came in through her kitchen door. 'Now I have to chuckle a little. I thought I had better come to the waiting room until he opens, Petter there.' And he sat down on the bench in front of the window and chewed tobacco and kept turning his head to see if there was any light over in the store. Sat there in his big, blue, homespun sweater, with his cap in his hand. He usually had a little syrup pot with him when he came to shop. He put it down on the window ledge.

And if no one else came to Petter's, he took his syrup pot and cap and said thank you and went home. He would rather come again later in the day and make another try at it.

One Christmas Eve Ludvik and Johan came together past Petter's living-room window. The women had gotten everything ready for the holidays. There was a Christmas tree in the living room with glass decorations; with flags and a spire on the top. And in between the decorations there were little *fattigmann* cookies hanging from sewing thread around their necks. 'Hu, hu, hu,' said Ludvik. 'There are an awful lot of 'poorman cookies' hanging on Petter's tree. Maybe he could hang me up, too!'

A Hand to Hold To

A lot of things changed in the twenties in Mostad. Sails and oars had to give way to motors. The contemporary world was knocking at the door. The skippers started to pull their eight-oared, five-man boats ashore, and bought fishing sloops. Or else they remodeled their five-man boats. Raised the clinker-built planking on the sides, nailed on a deck, and put in a motor.

But a boat like that was too heavy to pull ashore day after day. They had to have a harbor. And there was no harbor in Mostad. And no chance of making one, either, lying as they did, open to Vestfjord. Because of that, boat engines were a stab in the back to the Mostad community. The men had to move over to Vågen with their new boats for the winter season. They stayed in rented quarters all week long and came home on Saturday nights. Mostad had gotten its weekend commuters.

Johan Nicholaisa was one of the first to abandon his eight-oared, five-man boat. He went into partnership with Amandus, in Vågen, and bought a fishing sloop from near Bodø. It was named *The Cod*. They spent a couple summers in Sulitjelma working in the mines in order to scrape together the money for the payments.

The tiny, white-painted sloop had both a wheelhouse and a cabin, but the engine was always a question. The nameplate on the side of the green-painted motor said EASY, but it did not always live up to its trademark. They had to keep the monkey wrench within easy reach, especially when they lay on the Outer Bank in rough weather.

Amandus was an old captain, used to getting his way when he was on board. When EASY was difficult, he whacked it with his leather hat.

One time it was so bad that they had to be towed, in order to arrive safe and sound in port. Amandus went right to the telegraph office to send a dispatch to Bodø, to the man who had sold them the boat:

What's to be done
when EASY's mean?

The answer came:

Pull the piston,
scrape it clean;
the codfish catch
will soon be seen.

All winter long, at home in Mostad, the women took care of the children and the old-timers, and of life and death. If something came up during the week while the men lay in Vågen, it was they who had to set things straight. They had no contact with their husbands except for the occasional sight of their boats way out on the bay when they came in with the catch during the day.

But on Saturday nights, newly baked waffles were to be smelled all up and down House Brook Road, while the children stood in position down at the shore, waiting for the boats. It was a festive time when evening was coming on and the men were expected! The children followed the boats with their eyes all the way across the bay, from the time they rounded Kvalnes until they lay steadying themselves right outside the big landing. The boats were scarcely tied to the buoys before the boys were on board, clambering and climbing in the masts and the wheelhouses.

*

But it was not safe, every weekend, for the big sloops to lie at buoys outside the rocky Mostad beach. On such threatening weekends, the men came hiking over Håen, over the big mountain on the other side of the bay. That was the shortest way, when they had to come on foot. It took two hours in the wintertime.

In late winter when it became light enough, the children could stand on the shore and see the men like black dots against the eastern sky as they came in single file over the steep ridge. There was not much of a foothold up there. One step too far out to one side, and the fall was thirteen hundred feet straight down to the sandy beach. Were they to slip to the other side, it was head over heels down the steep mountain until they lay in the rocky debris by Røst Sea.

The children all knew that. They had heard about a fellow who had fallen one time. For that reason, it was always tense watching the column come down from the ridge. It never went quickly, because they always had heavy packs on their backs when they came from Vågen for their weekend visits. They carried fresh fish in their wooden backpacks. Fish for boiling for a week for the families at home.

When the column was almost all the way down, the boys ran across the field to meet them. They raced each other along the path between the hills and the rocks. The farther in they went, the narrower the little plain became. Mostad Mountain pushed out toward the bay and cut off the pasture land.

Up at the end, the mountain ridge forced the path down to the shore. It ran along the edge of the sea for the last hundred yards, along a rocky little beach. Mostaders called that little section the Beach Path. The boys had to stop there and wait. They did not have permission to go any farther. They could not walk across that little beach path unless there were grown-ups along.

In good weather, it was easy to travel along the edge of the shore. But when the men left their boats behind and came over the mountain, it was because the sea was too rough out on the bay. And when the bay was rough, it was rough by the isthmus, too. One had to be both very careful and light-footed to get across without getting wet. The sea poured in over the rocky path. Sometimes it filled up the whole shore and drove clear up the steep mountainside. The cliff was scrubbed clean twice the height of a man.

The sea has its moods. Everyone in Mostad knew that. A

large wave seldom came alone, and usually there were not more than three large waves in a row. So one simply had to count. When the third one was on its way out again, the Mostaders started to run and did not stop until they were safely up in the crevice that ran up the mountainside on the other side of the rocky beach, where they were safe.

The Climb was a crevice, slanted just enough so that they could find a foothold in it. There was a little shelter from the sea there, on the path. But if the sea were really rough, one had to run part of the way up into the crevice in order to avoid an unwanted bath. Sometimes the sea exploded all the way up the ravine and filled it.

Where the crevice ended, the path continued in little cutbacks up over a steep, grassy hillside. Where the grassy hillside ended, there was a steep, rocky headland. That was Stihalsen, the neck of the path, the needle's eye into Mostad.

The side of the mountain protruded right there, and pushed out between the grass-covered, vertical cliffs. There were several yards without a path, before one could again set foot on the ground on the other side of the mountain ridge.

It was a heavy rope that helped the Mostaders at Stihalsen. It hung from a bolt up on the mountainside. If they got a good grip on the end of the line, and placed their feet carefully, they could somehow manage the last few yards around the ridge. It wasn't necessary to ask twice for people to get a firm grip on the line. If their hands slipped, it was fifty yards straight down to the rocky beach.

The boys always had plenty to do when they stood at the edge of the Beach Path waiting for the company from Vågen. They had to wager which of the fathers would show up first on the rope up on Stihalsen. And when the first one had come into view, and let go of the line, it was impossible to agree who would be the next one.

When everyone was around, and they came zigzagging down the trail and were nearing the Climb, it was the sea the boys stood and kept an eye on. Sometimes the men did not get across the Beach Path fast enough with their heavy packs. And then they got a bath so that the salt water was running from them when they reached the crowd of boys.

As soon as the men were across, the boys became inquisitive and began to ask which of the crews had the best record that week. If somebody had made a real haul, there were always some in the group who took off running back south in order to be the first to come to the Homestead with the news.

But there were also those who stayed, and who found a hand to hold to. To come into the Homestead with Dad: that was something, too.

Eagles and Brandy

During spring and autumn and summer, the people in Mostad lived life as they always had. As soon as the Lofoten fishing was over, the men came home with their sloops and tied them up at the buoys. The two-man boats and the three-man boats were hauled out of the boathouses, and then there were oars and sails and small boats as before.

No one had as short a haul out to open sea as the men of Mostad did. They just had to go out the bay and around the point, and they were where the fish were, and could put out their handlines. When they had come home in the evenings with their catch, and sat at dinner, they could still see the Sørland boats out on the bay. They still had an hour's rowing ahead of them.

The years after the First World War were the leanest years in memory for Rookery Island. Inflation and poor fishing seasons, winter after winter, made life hard for most people. But in Mostad they did fairly well. They had birds on the mountain. Sea birds were a food reserve when things got tough. They could always find a few fish to cook, if they were patient enough. And most of them had domestic animals. Sometimes the fare was monotonous, but they didn't starve.

It was worse with things they had to buy. You had to have money to go to Petter's, and money was what there was very little of in Mostad, as on the rest of the island. For that reason, the twenties were relief-work years for the Mostaders, too.

From time to time they got a few kroner of government subsidy, so they were able to extend the path in toward the isthmus. With the subsidy, they were able to blast a shelf along the mountainside at the inner end of the bay, so they did not have to run a footrace with the sea along the Beach Path, and dangle on a line at Stihalsen.

They usually worked at it in autumn. They had a rest shed way back in the field, with a forge where they could sharpen their drills. Every morning a whole caravan of youngsters hiked back with lunchboxes for their fathers. And forgive the father who was so shamelessly hungry that he emptied the lunchbox! There had to be half a slice left in the bottom, so that the children could hold a party on the way home.

With the small amount of money they were given, they did not get very much blasted out from year to year. For that reason, their pride grew even larger as they neared completion. On the day that the breakthrough blast was to be set off, it was the girls who carried lunch to their fathers. There were waffles and lefse in the lunchboxes. And on the table in the workshed, they had laid out white tablecloths, with heather blossoms in jam jars.

It was no small thing to have a path all the way to the isthmus. You could see the midnight sun from up there, and a pasture half as large as Mostad Homestead itself. A whole world had been pulled a little closer for both grown-ups and children. There was nothing to be done about the fact that it still was a long way before the path led to *people*.

There was no end to what the new path might bring. One fine day, easygoing Sigurd came to the Homestead grinning from ear to ear. He had made a great discovery at the isthmus. He wouldn't say what it was.

But what Sigurd would not tell, Oluf and Johan discovered for themselves. As soon as it was possible to get away unseen from the Homestead, they set out inland to do a little investigating. Back of a large rock by the edge of the sea, they found more than they had dared hope for. There lay a fifty-five-gallon keg of French brandy just waiting for someone to tap it.

It seemed to them no more than fair that Sigurd should share with others, so they requisitioned the whole consignment on the spot. They managed to roll the keg over sticks and stones to a pile of driftwood. They buried it as deeply as they could under broken planks and box boards and Russian timber. Then they had to get hold of some tools so they could open the bung, and get some empty containers so they could start to carry the loot home.

But Oluf and Johan were not long in paradise. Other Mostaders got wind of the business, and new raids were launched against the formerly ever-so-peaceful isthmus. The keg kept shifting ownership, and was actually the property of Sigurd again at one time. No one was successful in concealing it for very long. There was a limit to how many hiding places there were for a fifty-five-gallon keg on a pasture between a mountain wall and the sea. It was never very clear who had confiscated it from whom, but all of them were blissfully happy, carrying the contents home in pots and buckets.

Fifty-five gallons was a lot, especially during Prohibition. The women took very little, and there were not many grown-ups in Mostad who would admit coming to the Homestead with brandy in buckets. Some were afraid of the sheriff, others of their wives, and some of the Lord. And the fact of the matter was that there was a limit to how much little Mostad could drink.

The most troublesome were the fellows from Nordland who were looking for the keg. They roamed regularly up and down the pasture out by the isthmus, and dug around in the driftwood. If the Mostaders did not carry the contents off soon, it was liable to fall into the hands of the enemy.

It was Oluf's idea that they might be able to make a little money from the brandy. The Sørlanders lived on the inner side of the island, and seldom found anything worth talking about on their shore. They ought to be pretty good customers. No sooner said than done!

But the Mostaders had not made many trips over to the bay at Sørland before everything went wrong. The sheriff came to make an inspection and a search of their houses. 'Flatland devil!' growled Oluf when he saw the boat out on the bay. Oluf did not have any stronger expression in his arsenal.

Before the official had set foot on land, the Mostaders had laid plans for their campaign. They could recognize the sheriff's boat a mile away! That gave them time to make a decision. If one of them would take the responsibility, the others would chip in and pay the fine. It was better to pay one fine than to pay many. It was a kind of federal budget they were agreeing on.

They chose Oluf to run interference, and that was all right with him. There was no way he could get by with paying less, he reasoned. So when the sheriff had boarded his boat and left, Oluf went into the sheep shed and took another snort. The sheriff had not looked in the cow barn under the grate to Dokka's manure pit. There was still enough of the sea's bounty left for several days of the Gay Twenties life along House Brook Road.

The next Saturday night the men stood on the Heap down by Martines's boathouse with lots to talk about, and with one thing or another hidden behind the boathouse wall. As they were standing there, with their heads together, Johan came staggering down through the Homestead with Oluf in tow. Both of them were dressed for the sea. Oluf rolled from side to side. He had one rubber boot on and another under his arm. They had decided to take a little trip out fishing, they had!

Martines came down from his house and asked if they were taking anything to drink with them. No! It was gone, they were sorry to say! And now they were going to try out the handline fishing, as well as they could. Martines thought they would be safe enough. In his opinion, rowing would sober them up.

They got the boat onto the water and clambered aboard. Johan decided to row, and took the oars. Before they were out of the landing, Oluf was dozing off in the stern.

On land, the men grinned and watched them make their way down the bay.

The next morning, it was Johan and Oluf who were grinning. Riding a fine southerly breeze, they came in at a good clip and swung their boat into the big landing so full of fish that it was difficult to remember when anyone in Mostad had ever had such a fine fishing trip.

***

The law had stopped the export of brandy across the bay. Oluf had his extra income, nevertheless. Above the swarming world of birds over the mountain at Mostad, the eagle circled on wide, quiet wings. When it was hungry, it slid down to the surface of the sea and impaled a mealtime fish on its needle-sharp claws. Or else it aimed for a carcass on the side of the mountain and chased away the ravens who had showed the way to the food.

But sometimes it was into the trap of Oluf Berntsa that the king of the birds landed. Oluf was the eagle man in Mostad. He may not have been the only eagle catcher, but he was easily the most zealous.

From the time that the darkness of autumn began, until Christmas, he kept at it. Every morning, before anyone was to be seen in the Homestead, he scurried up the mountain trail on coarse-stockinged feet. With a barn lantern in his hand and a pack with bait on his back. The point was to get to the place before it was light, so the eagle would not see that he was getting ready up there.

He had his hideout on the outer side of the mountain. It was built of stone, and covered with sod and moss so that it would blend into the side of the mountain. There was just enough room inside so that he could sit up and stretch out his legs when he sat on the floor. There was a hole in the roof just large enough so that he could get his stomach down through it. When he was finally inside, he pulled a slab of stone over the opening. He sat there all day long, until it was dark enough for him to creep unseen back down again. He sat on a layer of hay with a piece of blanket around him, and waited as he squinted out through a peephole in the side of the stone wall.

The peephole was big enough so that he could pull a full-grown eagle in through the side by the legs. Outside there was a flat stone slab. The bait lay there, an arm's length away from the hole. Usually it was a piece of sheep's carcass he had brought. It had to be large enough for the eagle to stand on when he ate. All around the piece of meat he had fastened a piece of line. When the eagle landed to have dinner, Oluf came to life inside the cave. Carefully he picked up the line, and even more carefully he pulled the eagle and the bait nearer the peephole. While the king of the birds gorged itself on the mutton, feeling at ease and in no danger, Oluf made his play.

As soon as the bait had been pulled near enough, he stuck his lightning-quick hands out through the opening and grabbed the eagle's feet. One jerk, and the eagle was in the hut. While it was still paralyzed from shock, Oluf pushed his knee into the eagle's side and wrung its neck. He knew it had to happen quickly if he were to avoid a life-and-death fight.

It was possible for Oluf to have five or six eagles in his bag when the day was done. That represented a few kroner from the sheriff. And if he were lucky, he would find someone who wanted to buy the wing or tail feathers for whiskbrooms. Catching eagles was a fairly steady income, and anyway, it was safer to sit in his eagle hut than to row a small boat in late autumn, with handgear . . .

English Daisies

Magda had a little garden in front of her house. It wasn't very big, but people in Mostad thought it was worth visiting. There were red peonies and yellow tiger lilies; there were poppies and English daisies and forget-me-nots. Summer after summer they had seen her bent over her flower beds. She had planted and sown until it was the purest Garden of Eden.

But best of all, people thought, were the narrow little paths. Magda had been across the bay with the Faroese boat and brought back chalk-white sand in buckets and pails. And every spring she rowed across again and got more so that the paths would really shine when the first blossoms unfolded.

A mountain ash raised its proud head along the south wall. It was so close to the kitchen window that when the window was open they could touch it with their hands. Magda planted the ash the year after she had come to Mostad. Her father had sent a box with the roots to her. He knew how much she liked everything that grew, and she had written to him and said how she had come ashore on a bare plain by the edge of the sea.

Over the years, there came to be three trees in Magda's forest. Right in the middle of the garden, on the tiny little patch of grass in front of the house, the bark of a crooked little birch gleamed white. That was the courtyard tree.

Closest to the ocean, a stubborn willow hung on for dear life. It was too far away from the house wall to get any protection from the north wind. It got pretty hard treatment in the winter when the gusts came sweeping in across the isthmus and threw themselves south along the bay and into the Homestead. Precisely where the north wind hit Mostad, there stood the willow.

But as soon as the wind shifted south, the willow was resurrected. Just as the north wind had laid it flat on the ground toward the south, now it was pressed down toward the north. And when there was no wind, it stood there, straight up, and leaned neither to one side nor the other.

Magda was proud of her garden; proud when Mostaders came to look at it. She enjoyed knowing that she had gotten something to grow where so little had grown before.

The flowers were pretty enough, she thought, but she liked the trees best of all. They had come from her home, from Tuv. They reminded her of another life than that in Mostad. They caused her to think about her childhood days, and about the life of a girl herding goats among the broad birch meadows and gleaming mountain lakes. They reminded her of the days when she did not fear the mountains, and was not anxious about the sea.

Magda's first cow was named Storma. She was flecked white across her back, and red along the sides. She had horns and was a very good milk cow. As soon as Magda came into view in the pasture, she came running and mooing so loudly that she could be heard a long way off.

The flock of sheep was large, and carefully tended, and they had all kinds of names. There was the Virgin, and the Miss and the Mermaid and Snow White. And big old Brownie, who had gotten her name because she had such brown eyes.

Magda thrived with all of them, and treated all of them as if they were her next of kin.

And so it happened one morning that she was doing the morning chores. She sat on the stool with the milk pail between her knees, and her red-plaid-bandanna-covered head against the side of Storma. It was so nice to rest her head like that against the warm side of the cow's body, and listen to the streams of milk as they sang their way into the pail.

Then there stood a neighbor woman in the barn doorway.

'You have to hurry and come. Lise is having a baby, and there is no one to help her!'

'You want me to come?'

'Yes. There is no one else. You have to come.'

Magda put the milk pail aside and went into the house and pulled off her barn clothes. Then she ran through the door and up House Brook Road with her hair clasp in one hand and a newly washed white apron in the other.

It was a strong little boy. Everything went well with the birth, and Magda became Mostad's new midwife. Or 'the labor woman,' as they called those who had not had a formal education as midwives.

She had begun as a midwife for animals. As a young girl in Tuv, she had to take care of everything by herself with the goat herd. She had not been in Mostad long before the Mostaders discovered her knack for animals. That is how they began to come and get her. And Magda came and helped. She might stay the whole night and try to get a calf from a cow, or a lamb from a ewe.

They had had a labor woman in Mostad before. That had been Kristen-Birgitte. When she began to get really old, they began to come to Magda well beforehand and ask if, when the time came, she could be there with Birgitte and give a hand if necessary.

One day, there was no Kristen-Birgitte anymore. No one doubted that Magda should take over. People and animals, it was all the same principle, they thought. And Magda had practiced for so long in the barn that she must be experienced.

Birgitte had helped bring eighty-some children to birth in her time. Not many years had passed before Magda had helped her first dozen to life. It was not a matter of stealing away the livelihood of the District midwife. She did it because she had to. It was not always possible to travel across the bay when children were born in the Homestead. Therefore it was necessary for the Mostaders to be self-sufficient with regard to giving birth, too.

And for that reason, it was usually during the bad weather that Magda had to be out helping with giving birth. When it was really bad, the house stood and shook in the blasts of the gale while Magda helped give birth up in the loft. Almost always, it roared and howled outside the house walls. Magda had music to help give birth by.

They came at all times of night and day and got her. She lay in the loft in a downpour one windy November night, with influenza and a fever of 104 degrees. She woke because someone stood pounding on the loft door, wanting to come in. Before she could get herself together enough to answer, the door opened and a man came in and posted himself at the foot of the bed, with a barn lantern in his hand. The rainwater ran down off his yellow oilskins. There was a small pond on the floor around his rubber boots.

'You have to come!'

'No, I can't come. I'm sick.'

'You can't say no!'

There was nothing more to say. Magda raised herself up in the bed, heavy with fever, and promised to get dressed and come. Come and sit. Then they would have to try to get the district midwife to come.

During the morning, the weather eased off enough for them to get a boat into the water and go for the midwife. But by the time the midwife landed in Mostad, the child was already born. There was only the postnatal care for her to do.

Magda staggered home along Brook Road in a delirium of fever. There was daylight over Håen in the east. A new day: time to go to the barn. She was the only one in the house to take care of the barn chores. Johan was gone on construction work.

*

One day there came a message from Sørland. The doctor and the midwife were stranded by weather on Røst. There was no one else to help except Magda in Mostad.

She got a ride across the bay in a fishing sloop. The weather was windy, and nasty, and so dark that they barely found their way into the Sørland landing. There they heaved to, and put a small boat onto the water. Magda clambered over the rail and was rowed to land. It was midnight and all the houses were dark except one. She groped her way along the rocky cart-road. She had a shopping bag in her hand. In it were a pair of scissors and a white apron, and some crocheting yarn that she used to tie the navel cord.

It was a poor home she had come to. She was busy all night at the couch in the tiny kitchen. There was not enough food in the house to prepare anything. She had to go to the neighbor's house to get a cup of coffee in the morning, before she could be taken back across the bay again, for another day in Mostad.

The job was not always over for Magda when the child had come into the world. After the birth, she often went on daily visits for a week or two, doing the dishes and housekeeping. She gladly did a clothes-washing or two, also, although she had more than enough to do in her own home. During the twenties, both Maren and Edvard had come to need nursing care. She had become bedridden with arthritis, and he had had a stroke and just sat in a chair.

Magda never asked for payment when she went to assist at birth. But sometimes it happened that when Lofoten fishing was over, one or another of the fathers would come and give her ten kroner. It was thanks for helping at childbirth.

She did not care much about the money. Johan was a good provider, and earned what they needed for their livelihood. She thought it was payment enough to be able to help bring a child into the world. 'People get to have babies only once. There is nothing to do but help them,' she said.

It was satisfying to come home when everything had gone well. But when it hadn't, she felt it deeply, and often for a long time.

When it was a poverty childbirth, she took some of the little she had in the dresser drawer, and gave it. A little clean linen to start life with: every child should have that.

Then tuberculosis came to Mostad. It was right in the middle of the twenties. First, Oluf Berntsa was made a widower. Edith, the daughter of Anna, south in the Homestead, was the next one the sickness took. She was the one who was going to be sent to America, and who never got away from the Homestead at all. She had a few childhood years, and then it was over.

After that, it happened thick and fast. Before long, more than twenty Mostaders were sick. Barely half of them survived. One autumn, four died within a few months. One family lost three children.

Again, it was to Magda people came for help. It often happened that she was there before they managed to come and get her. The veterinarian and the midwife became a nurse, too. She was always calm, no matter what happened, and that made everyone feel secure just to have her in the house.

'Oh, we'll manage somehow,' she said, however bad it looked.

She soon had a fixed route along House Brook Road, doing the washing and caring for those who had tuberculosis. People were seriously afraid of the sickness. Patients were often placed in a room in the loft where they were left alone. Walking down the road, one could see pale faces behind several attic windowpanes. A girl or a boy who could not bear to stay in bed, coming to the window to watch life in the Homestead.

Magda went to see all of them. When Oluf's wife was on her deathbed, Magda was there. And when Oluf was left alone, she continued to come. She sewed and did the wash and cooked for him and the three children he had been left with. The last night Edith was alive, it was Magda who sat at the end of the bed. When it was time to place Edith into a casket, it was Magda who took care of that, too.

It was not that the rest of the women in Mostad sat with their hands in their laps doing nothing. As soon as the tuberculosis had started to devastate the homes, they founded and organized a Tuberculosis Society. 'Help from Mostad' is what they called it. A schoolteacher got them started, and Magda was the chairman.

Actually, they already had one society in Mostad. That was the Missionary Society. It collected money for missions to the heathens, both for those at home and in places like China. But there was no reason why they could not hold double membership.

There was not that much difference in the way their meetings were conducted, anyway. There was prayer before and after each of the meetings, and hymns and knitting done in the TB Meeting as well as in the China Meeting. There was this difference: that the Missionary Society was subject to Our Lord, whereas the TB Society took its orders from Incognito Street in Oslo, where the headquarters of the National Society for Public Health was located.

Every two weeks Magda headed out the door with her guitar in her hand and the agenda under her arm. The meetings rotated among the members, so everyone's living room got an airing. Otherwise they were used only at Christmas and Easter.

As soon as they assembled, they read some Scripture. Then the coffee cups were put on the table. Then Magda pulled out the

Health News and the brochures from the agenda, and read aloud about cleanliness and the danger of infection and how to care for the sick, and how other societies in other places operated. After that they talked about the health situation in Mostad; where the need was the greatest and help most needed.

But they could not do much without money. They regularly sent people to the sanatorium in Salten, and it took money for the tickets and clothing and the stay. They needed woolen blankets and cure coats, too. Some people called them 'house coats.' They were nice, in any case. Nicer than anything Mostaders were used to. In Mostad they wore their winter underwear or a slip. One either slept, or was up and properly dressed.

They often had lotteries at their meetings. They drew for trifles they had made, or cakes they had baked. That produced a few kroner. But, if it were going to be of much help, they had to have bigger projects.

It was the big annual auction that really raised money. It was held in July, when the fishing was over and people still had a little money in their hands.

All winter long there was knitting and crocheting, and the later it got in the spring, the busier it got for Magda and her troops. The last few days before the festival, there was chatter about baking and cooking in every kitchen. Yards of wheat cakes that could be cut up and sold with coffee and chocolate, and liter after liter of stewed prunes and almond pudding.

Then there was nothing to do but hope for good weather. When it was good, sloop after sloop loaded to the gunwales with people came from Sørland and Nordland and Vågen. Sometimes the harbor lay chock-full of boats. The TB Festival in Mostad was 'notorious.'

It began at five o'clock on a Saturday afternoon. At that time the flag was hoisted to the top of the school flagpole. In the schoolroom everything was decorated and ready. There were long trestle tables along two walls, and white tablecloths. Bunches of flowers burst out of jars and vases, and on the blackboard it said WELCOME in big chalked letters. All along the edge of the tables, the Mostad community's collection of coffee cups paraded in assorted ranks.

But there was no sipping of coffee until the auction was over. Johan, Magda's husband, was the auctioneer. He had been the foreman on a blasting crew, and when he got a little too enthusiastic, he sometimes forgot himself and shouted, 'HEADS UP!' as he was about to pound his carpenter's hammer down on the piece of board he had laid on the lectern to protect the paint.

He played the crowd as well as he could. Pitted the Sørlanders against the Nordlanders when they bid, and the Mostaders against the people from Vågen. No one wanted to be a cheapskate. They sold baskets and packages and bags. They were varied in style and size and decorations, but every one of them had food in it. A thigh of mutton, butter from a cow, a stack of bread slices covered with mutton sandwich meat, ready for consumption. Or a packet of lefse. With every hammer blow Johan made at the lectern, more kroner flowed into the tuberculosis treasury.

The men who were farsighted enough took care of their winter clothing needs. On a line along the wall there were stockings and mittens and thick overstockings lined up one after the other. There was clothing for the women, too. One year Petter had a bolt of red woolen cloth on the shelves of his store. That year there was a red apron from every other house, making the clotheslines brighten up all around the auction room.

There was suspense among the women when Johan started to auction things off. In every package of food there was a piece of paper with the name of the woman who had prepared it. It was the custom for the buyer to treat the preparer of the food to coffee. When Johan had put his hammer down, and everything was sold, it was time to locate the woman who had done the baking, and find a place to sit on a bench.

Then Magda and the other TB ladies came with treats and teased a few more kroner out of them. The stewed prunes went for twenty-five øre a bowl, and the almond pudding for the same amount. *Rømmekolle* brought the most. The visitors paid whatever was asked for the bowls of cultured cream. It was not possible to leave the TB Festival in Mostad without having tasted the Mostaders' exceptional *rømmekolle*.

As the evening wore on, the boys and girls became restless, and when the food table had been emptied, they went in a group up to the dance platform out on the field. Someone always brought an old accordion along to the TB Festival in Mostad. And if there was none, there were always those who had a harmonica in their back pockets on a Saturday night in July.

The drawback to the dance platform was that it was made of concrete and was as rough as an emery wheel. No one was able to dance for very long. The surface ground their holiday shoes to shreds. But however long it was, sooner or later everyone found someone, and wandered farther back toward the isthmus and the midnight sun. There was plenty of room in the soft grass down by the sea.

There were those who found their lifetime companions on such nights. It was not every day that a swarm of young men and young women from Sørland and Nordland and Vågen came together on the stony fields of Mostad. One had to strike while the iron was hot. And that happened when it was summer, during the TB Festival.

Full Sails

The schoolhouse was the work of Petter Kristensa. Since the turn of the century, the tall, white-painted building with the overly large windows lying north in the Homestead had been a place both for education and for festivals.

Earlier, the Mostaders had to travel to Nordland if they wanted to learn to add or subtract. Gradually, as the number of children increased, the demand for a school in the Homestead became more common. But the county had a lean treasury, and said no.

The only thing they got was a teacher who came for a few weeks each autumn and conducted lessons around a baking table in someone's kitchen. Then it was that Petter finally took the matter into his own hands. He rowed over to the county chairman and said that if no one else would build a schoolhouse, then *he* would do it. And such an offer was hard to refuse. A contract was written, to the effect that Petter would build the schoolhouse for two thousand kroner, and that the county would pay him back in reasonable amounts when they had the means to do it. The county chairman thought it was a dangerous gamble with official funds. 'That Petter from Mostad will bankrupt the county,' he said. He was one of those from western Norway, down by Bergen.

The school rose into the air so fast that it was ready for use before the furniture had come. They went and got the baking table they had been using and placed it right in the middle of the floor. The boys sat on a long bench on one side, with the girls on the other. Petter's wife volunteered herself as an unpaid janitor, and took on the job of making the fire and doing the washing when the teacher came and school was in session. They had to share him with Sørland, so school was held for only fourteen days at a time.

At Christmas they heated up the schoolhouse and had a festival. First for the children, and then it was the grown-ups' turn. People came dressed in their best, carrying not only food, but chairs and tables as well. After devotions and Scriptures, coffee was served, followed by the dance around the Christmas tree.

Just as they were dancing around the tree in two circles in opposite directions, Oluf came steaming in from the cold. He had been out and had just the slightest glow on.

'Oh my, oh my! The tree is going to tip over!' he shouted, and broke his way through both the outer and the inner circles of dancers with that great round stomach of his.

People didn't get too excited, because Oluf tended to act like that every year at the Christmas Festival. As soon as he had fought his way in to the tree, he turned his back on it and began to direct the carols, and the way they were dancing around him and the tree.

Oluf was not the type to disgrace a Christmas tree, however wonderfully decorated it was. He wore his bridegroom's suit when he went to the Christmas Festival. 'The Thirty-Year-Old,' he called it. He used the suit only once a year.

The dark blue, homespun jacket was large and loose-fitting, and had broad lapels and big outside pockets. A striped, round shirt collar with a collar button in the back stuck up at the neck. He always wore a visored cap with it, whether inside or outside, and he wore black, shiny rubbers on his feet. Oluf's weakness in life was galoshes. He had a large stock of them, and arranged them according to their shine.

When they had sung all the verses of all the Christmas carols, and it began to get warm up under the roof and inside the undershirts, it was time for the mixed choir. They had been in hard training twice a week all autumn in preparation for Christmas – the only time of the year they held an indoor concert.

They arranged themselves around the lectern platform, and the director got the pitch from an old fiddle he used for that purpose. Then they tuned up with songs from the *Evangelistic Hymnal* and *Zion's Harp*. 'I have sunken deep in sin, Far from the peaceful shore.' 'Throw the lifeline on the water, Where a brother needs our hand.'

But the mixed choir reached its peak, as most folks saw it, when they got to the patriotic songs and began to sing about Ulabrand and Olav Tryggvason: 'At sea where he worked, There he sank one day.' 'Full sails blow along North Sea shores.'

Bernt and Elvine were two of the most enthusiastic choir members. Bernt had grown up as a foster son to Martines, together with Martines's first family. After he grew up, the two often rowed as partners. Bernt dropped in every day, even after he had married and had his own family.

They had a total of thirteen children, he and Elvine. But

childhood sicknesses were the rule in their house. Before the thirteenth one had been born, five had died.

There were enough left for them to have their own little mixed choir around the kitchen table. He sang bass, and she alto, and the children filled the scale all the way from toothless da-da-da up to where their voices changed. Even when they were tired from doing the haying all day, they sang in the evening before they went to the loft to bed.

The only trees in Mostad were in Magda's garden, and she guarded them carefully. Leafy trees don't make very good Christmas trees, anyway. Up at the schoolhouse, and at Petter's, they bought trees. Everyone else in the Homestead made Christmas trees. They took a stick or a broomstick and tied heather branches on it with wire. They cut angels from the silvery paper from bars of baking chocolate, and they put cotton wool on the clumps of heather. If the autumn had not been altogether bleak, there might be a few heart-shaped paper baskets with a few raisins.

On Christmas Eve morning, the wooden tub was carried into the kitchen, and there, one after the other, they took their turns with soap and a scrub brush. When they had dried, holiday clothes were put on and everyone was sent into the living room. At two o'clock there was lutefisk and flat bread·all over the Homestead, followed by coffee. There weren't many packages. The gifts were mostly the new clothing they were given when they came up out of the tub.

At Elvine and Bernt's, it was the package from Oslo that made Christmas. They had a daughter who worked at a wholesaler's in the capital city, and every Christmas a package came. When he wore his Christmas suit, Bernt was the most elegant man in the Homestead. He wore a diplomatic overcoat that had come from down south, one year.

The Oslo package usually came a few weeks before Christmas, and put the whole flock of younger children to a severe test of patience. The minute their parents left the house, they sneaked in and out of the living room, tugging at the string, turning the label over, and trying the package for weight.

One year Bernt got a long pipe. That was easy to guess. It wasn't even necessary to shake the package.

'You don't know what you're getting! You don't know what you're getting!' they teased him.

'It's nice to have a surprise,' chuckled Bernt.

Three days before Christmas Eve, he woke the oldest boy, Ingolf, up in the loft, and said that he should get dressed so they could row out with the handgear and catch some Christmas fish.

Elvine was already sitting at the kitchen table, sewing. There were still some clothes to get ready for the holiday. Bernt cautiously stole a peek through a crack in the door and said goodbye before he went down to the landing: 'Elvine, dear, I left my wallet. There are a few coins in it, if you should need any buttons or anything for your sewing there.'

During the morning, a norther came up on the Outer Bank. When evening approached, and they still had not come back to land, Elvine put on her coat and went to sit on the headland. There was nothing to see except a white breaker every time the sea heaved itself up over the rocks.

Bernt and Ingolf never returned to land. But on Christmas

Day, when the Mostaders were on their way to church, they found the boat in the rocks outside Nordland.

★★★

Elvine had animals in the barn, and children who were old enough to lend a hand. And what they could not do themselves, other people in the Homestead helped them with. She never talked about what had happened. But many years later, after she had died, they found a few lines in a dresser drawer that she had written herself, the winter Bernt and Ingolf were lost:

> *Now he is gone, my loving man.*
> *He was my happiness, and he was my life.*
> *I go lonesome here now on the earth,*
> *and only God knows how much I grieve.*

> . . .

> *Oh, Ingolf my son, why did you have to die,*
> *at such a young age on such a horrible sea?*
> *Oh, God, what pain there is in my breast,*
> *when I think of you, my blessed child.*

> . . .

> *You have your five brothers and sisters up there,*
> *If I knew you would be gathered with them*
> *then the sorrow would not be so deep*
> *for your surviving mother and family.*

'What will we two do?' Martines had sighed as he sat on the porch steps, without his sons, and alone. The housekeeper, standing behind him, promised to stay with him always.

Not many years passed before Martines found a solution. He went to the pastor and got a marriage license for himself and the housekeeper. Her name was Lise, and she was thirty years younger than he.

So Martines started all over again. In ten years six children were born, the youngest when he was seventy. He named the first three boys Alfred, Thorvald, and Frithjof after the three he had lost.

For the children, Martines was both a father and a grandfather. He was as easygoing and good-natured as he had been with his first brood.

When they were together in the hay fields in the summer, the little boys used to play pranks on the old man. They had fun hiding behind the balls of hay and hanging on when he tried to lift them. 'Oh,' he used to chuckle, 'I think I have lost all my strength.' And then the boys began to laugh, and their little scheme was uncovered.

And Martines used to munch forever on toasted bread crusts when he was in the hay fields. He didn't smoke, and he didn't chew tobacco, and he didn't use snuff. He thought it was only reasonable, then, that he have a toasted breadcrust to suck on. He used to go in to Lise in the kitchen and get a handful of *skorper* to stick into the pocket of his overalls before he went up onto the mountain.

Martines loved children, but his patience had its limits, nevertheless. An old braided boat fender hung in the entryway. That was his paddle. It did its job best just by hanging there. It seldom came to the point of bare bottoms. When the children were in an uproar in the kitchen, and they saw Martines rise and go toward the entry door, they knew that things were getting dangerous. And since the entry door was blocked by Martines and the boat fender, they ran for the loft and hid themselves.

Martines stamped up the stairs with the disciplinary knot of line in his hand, but when he got up to the loft, there were no sinners to be seen anywhere. Then he had to go down again to the kitchen to get the matchbox to see who was hiding under the bed. But as quickly as Martines had gotten the match down below the edge of the bed and tried to look underneath, a child's mouth would appear and blow it out. Martines took out a new match, but it never went any better with the next one. It could go on like that until there were smiles both above and below the bed.

One time when Martines was hunting for family criminals on his knees on the loft floor, Oluf Berntsa suddenly appeared at the head of the stairs.

'Now, can you tell me, Martines, what you are doing in the sleeping loft with a boat fender?'

No, actually Martines could not do that. He raised himself up, brushed off the knees of his trousers, and with some embarrassment went down the steps and hung the fender back on the nail.

In Mostad, holy days were holy. On Sunday mornings, the Homestead was becalmed. No children were allowed outside.

There was no one to be seen other than the white-shirted men who stood in a group on the Heap down below Martines's house having a quiet morning conversation.

As the clock neared eleven, Martines strolled down toward the fellows. He stood there awhile, chatting, then he turned to his own sons and said: 'Now we are going up, boys!' They often managed to get home before him. They thought it was no fun to be picked up.

As soon as Martines had the troops in the house, he took the books down from the shelf. But before he began to sing the first hymn, he opened the window so that those who still remained on the Heap would hear the hymns and understand that now it was time for everyone to go home.

Martines had a voice that carried. He sang so that it could be heard all over the Homestead. He was a kind of church bell for all of Mostad. He sang the Homestead empty. From eleven to twelve, there was church in every house. The hymns lay like a veil over the neighborhood.

But, of course, there were some who did not obey. Instead of going home they sneaked up beneath Martines's window and had a kind of open-air High Mass.

At one o'clock, there was dinner. As soon as *that* was done, kids bounded out of every house. The small boys ran down to the shore and found their wooden boats between the rocks. The larger ones went up onto the mountain.

And those who thought of themselves as too big to go down to the shore, and still did not have permission to go up onto the mountain, managed to get into the mountains, anyway. Either they sneaked off with the big kids, or they *pretended* they were in the mountains. Pretended they were gathering the sheep. One would crawl up on a shelf a few yards above the field and pretend he was a sheep who had gotten trapped. Then the others would come with ropes around their shoulders ready to rescue. The 'sheep' would stand on elbows and knees and bleat and bleat, until it not only was rescued but, before the game was over, knocked on the head and slaughtered, as well.

But should a boat come across the bay bound for Mostad, they let the sheep stay where it was and scurried down the hill to the bay to stand on the outermost rocks of the landing as the stranger's boat drifted in toward land.

And the girls lived their own lives. The smallest ones ran from house to house with whatever they had for playing dolls, visiting each other. The oldest girls leaned on the stone fences and taught each other folk songs.

Late in the afternoon, after they had taken their naps, the men and the women began to move around. They went for walks, looking at things up and down House Brook Road and between the ridges back in the field. If the weather and the footing were good.

There was Oline, for instance, tall and thin, who usually had her ball of yarn fastened to her belt with a safety pin, and who knitted as she walked. There was Anna with a tiny little white apron on her stomach, and Ludvik in his fine cap, both of them fat and rolling like sailors. And always arm in arm on Sundays.

For Martines, every day was holy. He held morning and evening devotions all week long. When he had to go to sea, so that the time had to be shortened in the morning, he made up for the loss by making it longer in the evening. What he liked best was to sing hymns. He knew the tunes to most of the songs in the book.

In the evening, he could stand under the lamp in the kitchen and sing song after song, including all the verses to all of them.

The hymn book nearly disappeared inside his big knotted hands. They were as brown as tanned leather, with lines and furrows that made criss-cross patterns until they looked like a map of Europe. He wore an old pair of shoemaker's glasses on his nose. His boys had found them in a leather case down at the shore. Martines was not sure he could see any better when he wore them, but he used them when he read, anyway.

Martines was a cautious man. He had always been that way. So when he found himself being a provider for the second time, he worried that he would not be able to provide them with what they needed to live. But he never complained, and didn't like it when others did, either. When he heard somebody lamenting one thing or another, he always had something to say:

'No, you should just take it easy, now. We don't deserve anything better.'

But, even though Martines was always cautious, and never put himself in danger, either on land or on sea, fate seemed to put him nearby whenever anyone else needed help. Martines was the rescuer in Mostad. He had saved lives at sea three times. In the big storm in 1904, he had rescued people by taking down the sail and rowing up to a capsized five-man boat. On the day of the big disaster in 1910, it was he who had saved the last member of Ivar Ellingsa's crew. When Johan had been shipwrecked with the book salesman outside Kvalnes, it had been Martines who had come to the rescue.

The Municipal Board had passed a resolution that he should receive a medal. But it never amounted to more than a resolution. And it wasn't important, Martines thought. If anyone started to talk about a reward, he turned and walked away.

And so the lighthouse keeper on Rookery Island took charge. He thought it was not right that Martines did not get anything. He wanted him to be recognized, and arranged for Martines to get a year's free subscription to the *Lofoten Post*. But Martines said no. And he had been a subscriber for thirty years, if that was of any importance.

With the Flag Held Low

BE A SUNBEAM, it said on the school flag in Mostad. It was home-made from cheap silk, as blue as the Mediterranean. Two mountain peaks stuck up out of the horizon. The cleft between them exploded tomato-red with a midnight sun, half-set. Fiery yellow beams fluttered over the rim of the sun, making shiny paths on the sea, down toward the tassels along the bottom. Across the top someone with a fairly unsteady brush had painted: MOSTAD SCHOOL, Rookery Island. The flag was not used often, but on Constitution Day it was brought out and given an ironing.

Before the war, the 17th of May celebration had not been much in Mostad. The men were usually at sea, and the women had their own work to do. But the children each had a flag, and sometime in the afternoon there was usually a little parade along House Brook Road. The older ones dressed up and rowed over to the Sørland festival.

It was a few days before the 17th of May Festival in 1934.

Anna, south in the Homestead, had gone up to the loft to find the flag, to iron it and get it ready for their daughter, Nordis. But when Nordis saw the flag she began to cry. It was both tattered and faded. She wanted to have a new flag. Anna and Ludvik couldn't afford that, so Ludvik did his best to comfort her:

'This kind is the very best kind,' he said, 'because it shows how often they are used.'

The next day a small steamer with herring bait came to Vågen. Quite a few of the men from Mostad went across and bought bait, intending to make a few sets with their gear. Ludvik was one of them. He thought he might put out a couple tubs and earn a few kroner for the 17th of May. He had managed to get his head far enough above water to borrow enough money to buy a boat. A twenty-foot, white-painted boat with a little motor. The vessel was old and the engine was too small. When there was much wind, he would have to be towed in to land, even though he had a little foresail to help things along.

About dinnertime on the 16th of May he got ready to go out. He had Sigfred, his son from Nordland, with him so that there would be two of them in the boat. Anna stood in the basement baking flat bread as they were leaving. It was her fortieth birthday. Ludvik came to the outside basement door and said a few words to her just before he left:

'You will see now, if we can find a few fish, you will get a birthday present when we come back and sell the fish.'

The weather was fine as they left. But during the evening, a northeaster came blowing in over the Homestead, and hit so hard that the men had to run for Vågen with their sloops in order not to be driven up on the land and crushed.

When Nordis came down from the loft in the morning of the

17th of May, Ludvik and Sigfred had not yet returned to land. Anna paced around uneasily in the kitchen. She continually went over to the window and pulled the curtain aside.

But it had happened before that they had come late from the sea with the new boat. They did not have much horsepower to help them when the wind was against them. And she had heard from a neighboring woman along the road that there were other boats that had not returned, too.

After breakfast, she dressed Nordis for the 17th of May celebration. Put red ribbons in her yellow braids, and put on the blue striped dress and the white knitted stockings she had gotten ready. The parade was not going to be until later in the day, but Nordis wanted to leave right away, and took the flag and went.

★

At three o'clock there was a gathering at the school. There was already a flock of children there when Nordis came running in through the door. The flag was ready over by the wall. But the children were unusually quiet, and they became even quieter when Nordis came.

'Are you planning to be in the parade?' one of older schoolgirls asked.

'Yes, I surely am,' Nordis answered, bewildered.

'Don't you know that your father and your brother were lost at sea last night?'

'That's not true!'

'Go home and ask your mother, and you will see!'

And Nordis went home. 'It's not true, it's not true,' she said to herself as she tramped south along House Brook Road in her 17th of May finery. The flag dragged along behind her on the ground.

But it *was* true. When she got home, her mother was lying on the couch in the kitchen, staring at the ceiling. She did not cry, and she said very little.

She had just gotten a message from Vågen. All the Mostad boats were already in harbor except for one. A violent storm had caught them during the night. They had had to run before the wind, and had not been able to reach land until late in the day.

It was Pentecost before the weather let up enough for them to go out and search. They searched all the way down to Røst, but boat after boat came back without seeing anything.

The following summer a window from the wheelhouse drifted ashore near Mosken.

*

So Anna was on her own again. She had become a widow for the second time. She got twenty-five kroner a month in widow's pension, and twelve and a half kroner for Nordis. That just about bought coal for the winter.

Anna stretched the working day out still longer. It had always been long. She got up at four each morning and began to spin and knit and bake flat bread. She did not want to hear a word about welfare.

'We'll manage somehow,' she said. She was not worried about there being nothing. And something usually did turn up. People came south along the road, morning and evening, carrying pitchers of milk. One came in the morning, and another in the evening: it was a kind of relay. Those who did not bring milk came with potatoes and meat and fresh fish. 'Now we are going to bait a hook for Anna,' Oluf used to say when he was out with the handgear. Every once in a while Martines would stick a leg of mutton up under his sweater. He could not bear to think that someone in the Homestead would go without food. He did not want people to see that he was helping, either, but no one doubted the kind of errand he was on when he went south and had a larger chest than was reasonable.

It was not the lack of food, but the roof of the house that Anna worried about. She was always afraid it would blow off. When a storm came, she took Nordis and some bedding and went to Eldore's, in the middle of the Homestead, to sleep on the kitchen floor at night.

But finally it was the porch that went its way. It happened one winter night, several years after she had lost Ludvik. One northwest blast after another threw itself over the isthmus and the bay, and swept over the Homestead, leaving it looking like a battlefield. The sod roofs were stripped off the racks and boathouses, and flew through living-room windows so that the glass splintered. Flagpoles broke like matches, and sheets of corrugated iron cut through the air so that it was a danger to life to try to go out.

Before midnight it was dead calm again. The snow was dark with dirt and sod, and Anna was without a porch. Only the steps and the platform remained. Kettles and buckets and pieces of board were found the next day up beneath Tinden, several hundred yards away. During the summer, a fellow came down from the mountain with Anna's baking apron. He had found it in a hay field on the outer side of the mountain.

Ludvik's death brought about Anna's religious conversion. She thought she had had enough on her mind, without having to prepare to submit to God, too; but she was wrong.

'He came and called to me. So I had to make a choice. And that lasted until finally I had to give in.'

She had a little table in front of her living-room window. There was a rosemaled cheese platter there, an oval jam dish, and coffee services for two. One of the coffee services was white and delicate with a gold border. The other was violet with yellow and blue flowers. They were presents from her two weddings.

She never used the living room after Ludvik was lost. Even on Christmas Eve, she sat with Nordis in the kitchen. Saturday nights were the most depressing. That was the day the others had gotten their men back home.

The Bench

In spite of everything, the thirties were not as hard for most Mostaders as the twenties had been. The price of fish gradually rose, as well as there being a few more fish in the sea. There were a few good years, now and then.

For the government authorities on Rookery Island, though, everything went to fiscal hell. During all of those hard years, it had been impossible to collect taxes from people. A few good years were not enough to remove the poverty. Before the decade was over, the county was bankrupt.

In Mostad, things continued to change. More boats with engines were bought, until the last eight-oared, five-man boat was pulled up on shore for good. And they got telephones in the Homestead. But they did not come free.

There was very little to be gotten from the county treasury. If they were going to establish communications with the outside world, they would have to do it themselves. They sent neither a delegation to the county commissioner nor a letter to the Parliament: they set up a theater. And went on the road as a visiting troupe to the gymnasium in Sørland with a three-act play. If they were going to make any money for poles and wires, they had to go where the people were, and that was in Sørland.

They had been in heavy rehearsal in the schoolhouse all summer and autumn before they climbed on board their sloops and went across the bay with scenery and costumes and guitars. They even brought a prompter's box with them, but they had little need for it. The cast members had learned their lines by heart, just as if they were learning hymn verses for the pastor.

It wasn't so important how well people liked the play. They had no intention of repeating the performance. Once the people were inside the door, the money was theirs.

Before the curtain opened, there was a prologue, and it began like this:

Look at the eagle sailing high
Above our island's majestic height.
The small birds chirp from the crested peaks
Late on a sheltered summer night.

And so the way was cleared for the drama. The plot was domestic, and easy to identify with. A young girl had moved away and taken a job as a domestic when times were bad, and then there came a letter saying that she was coming home for Christmas with a baby. The parents were all upset, wondering what the neighbors would think, but nevertheless began to get things ready for the baby. The wife scurried around, confused, giving orders right and left. At nights the husband built a cradle by lamplight.

And then the daughter came with the local boat and stood in the living room in her hat and nice coat, and with a pink, squealing baby pig under her arm. She had wanted to surprise her parents, since it was Christmas and things were tough.

The father was so bewildered that he stumbled over the cradle, smashing it to smithereens. The audience in Sørland shrieked with pleasure, in competition with the pig. Success was in the bag when the actors went out to the bay about midnight. It was late in the autumn, and very dark, but they had the money – enough to get telephones.

The next summer the telephone poles came on a cargo boat from Helgeland. In the evenings, when the weather was good, the men came with their boats and towed them around Nordlandshagen and put them in place, one after the other out along the trail.

They had a party in the schoolhouse on the first day it was possible to lift the receiver and talk to the Sørlanders without seeing their faces. With a mixed choir, and brandy in their coffee, and a dance afterward.

They installed two phones in the neighborhood, one at Monrad's, south in the Homestead, and one at Petter's, up north. There was no thought about taxes and fees. When the wire blew down, they went out themselves and hung it up again, and that was free.

There were those who weren't so excited about telephones and newfangled technology. During the thirties, there were three old fellows who made their daily trips down to Magda's.

Magda could tell by the sound when it was Nikolai who was coming. He dragged one foot and used a cane, and always kicked off his wooden clogs in the entry before he knocked on the door. When he had gotten the all-clear signal, he always opened the door a crack and said, 'Good evening,' before he threaded that tall, thin figure in through the opening, shuffling across the floor in his thick-stockinged feet, and sat by the bench beneath the window. He was smooth-shaven, and bald.

Nikolai had worked as the bow man in a five-man boat all his life, and had a permanent place in the bow. So he always sat at one end of the bench, and never said any more than was necessary.

No sooner had Nikolai found his place, than there would be someone else in the entryway. That would be Oluf. As soon as he saw Nikolai on his way down to Magda's, he took his cap off the nail and set out, too.

'My goodness, imagine that! Nikolai is here, too,' he said to himself as he came in. '*Ja*, you live like rich Lazarus,' he usually added. But if Magda took too long to warm up the coffeepot, he became impatient: 'Well, it doesn't look like there is going to be anything to eat around here!'

Oluf had become as round as a barrel over the years, and though he might have been five different people before, he had not become any less complex with age. He still went up to his eagle's hideout, although he was over sixty. And he had properly brought up the most recent batch of kids, even though he had had to do it alone.

He was as clean-shaven as Nikolai, and had his hair cropped close. His clothing was always well cared for and orderly. He sewed and patched and kept everything in first-class shape. 'Oluf is the cleanest man in the Homestead,' the women used to say. He was so clean that he opened the stove lid when he spat out his tobacco.

Oluf hunched himself down in the middle of the bench, so that there would be room at the inner end, by the stove. That was Martines's place. He was the captain of that crew. If Nikolai sat in the bow, then it was no more than right that Martines sat in the stern. Anyway, he had a legitimate claim to the spot nearest the stove. He had been a regular guest at Magda's since she first came to Mostad.

Martines had never gotten to the age of motors. He lived in the old days, as he always had. He had grown up in the eight-oared boats, and when he could no longer manage that, he had found a four-oared boat to work on. It was small, and the fishing had not been terribly good, either. But he had some old fellows with him, so that at least there was someone to give orders to, from the seat in the stern.

He was seventy-seven before he retired. The responsibility to be a provider had rested on him. And he was stubborn, and did not want to give in. Finally, the others had to take over and get him out of the boat.

There were some difficult years for him after that. His boys were still too young to go to sea. He had seen no way out except to ask the local government for a loan of two thousand kroner for himself and his family. That had been a hard thing for Martines to do.

All three of them took a trip down to Magda's in the evening. They came and sat on the bench and got coffee and sugar bits. Oluf was too young to be counted in with the two eighty-year-olds, but he was single and alone and he, too, enjoyed a little woman's care.

Martines usually came last, and unobtrusively. He wore overalls in his old age. But the sheath knife hung in back as always. His beard had become white, and hung like a little stiff wreath around his neck. His broad face was as ruddy as it had always been.

'Sit down, Martines, and I will get you some coffee,' Magda said when he came.

'Oh, no!' he said, energetically waving his hand. 'Magda, don't make a fuss over me! You need what little you have!'

Even though Martines had become old, he was still Martines. Sometimes the fifty- and sixty-year-olds who sat in the boathouse playing cards on Sunday evenings stuck the cards up under their jackets when Martines came walking by. Although he had never said a word, either about playing cards or anything else. In Martines's house, there was room for God, and a drink, and an eight of hearts, too.

But he always went to church when there was a pastor in the pulpit and the weather was good enough to get across the bay. They had gotten a church in Sørland in the thirties. The boys had to row him across. In church, he always sat in the same place in the back, and sang with a voice powerful enough to be heard in every corner.

The Eighth Army

The bird mountains filled, and emptied, and filled again. Swarming life became an oppressive stillness, and after the stillness, more swarming again. The years went that way. Then the war came to Mostad.

On the evening of the 8th of April, northern weather settled in over the Homestead with a storm and driving snow. Swept in over the houses and boathouses and drying racks and made House Brook Road into a swirling, impassable perdition of snow. Down south, Tinden blocked the wind. From there, the wind was thrown back and down into the Homestead again. Right in the middle of the crossfire the Mostaders sat around their kitchen tables and worried that they would all be made homeless.

Early the next morning a woman came and rapped on Magda's window:

'Now you have to turn on your radio. Something terrible is happening!'

Before ten o'clock in the morning, the men were home from Vågen with their sloops. They had not dared go out with their longlines. There were warships in Vestfjord.

Before the first week of the war had ended, Mostad had lost its only soldier. His name was Bjarne, and he was killed by a bomb near Narvik.

After that, it was the sea mines that were a threat to the Mostaders. Regularly, during the years of the war, the mines came drifting into the bay and settled into the rocks right by the path up by the isthmus. Johan had an old Krag-Jørgensen rifle in the house that he had hidden from the Germans. Because of it, they were put in charge of mines. They hid behind a crag and fired away. It did not do much good the times they tried, and soon they were out of ammunition.

So they had to notify the sheriff. But before his men came to blow it up, the Mostaders went in with monkey wrenches and pipe wrenches and unscrewed the shackle and chain and everything movable on the mine. It was not every day that mooring chain came drifting on the sea.

One morning Magda was awakened by someone going along House Brook Road shouting:

'You have to get up. There is a big mine drifting in toward land!'

Magda sounded the alarm and got everyone in the house on their feet. Johan went to the window toward the sea and peeked out. The mine was so close that Magda was not even allowed to cook coffee before they had to get out of the house.

There were a few mounds above the road. They provided a kind of protection should the mine go off. They led the old folks and the children up there from all over the Homestead. In their hurry, some lost their wooden shoes, others their caps. Most of them knew so little about warfare that they smiled and laughed as they climbed up through the grass and rocks.

While everyone else evacuated up behind the mounds, two men went to the landing and launched a three-man boat. That was Alfred, Martines's son, and Ulrik. The houses were crowded so close to the shore that they wanted to stop the mine before it reached the rocks.

While people lay in hiding, stretching their necks to see what was happening on the bay, Ulrik and Alfred slipped up close to the mine and got a line fastened to a ring on it. Then they rowed hard, towing the abomination out. They tied it to a metal pole on a reef outside the Homestead, and left it there temporarily.

During the day the wind shifted and became a little more westerly. Then they rowed out again and let it go so that the wind and the current could do the rest. About dinnertime there was an explosion in the rocks way up the bay. The flames shot way up the side of Håen, and the windows rattled and the saucepans danced all over Mostad Homestead.

★★★

Magda had just gotten a new Philips radio when the war broke out. The old radio receiver was not of much use any longer.

Then the orders came to turn in all radios. One after the other they went in boats to turn in their radios to the sheriff's office. Magda rowed herself over with her Philips case. But inside she had placed the old receiver. The new radio was hidden up in the loft.

That is how it happened that she was the only one in Mostad with a radio during the war. She traded a little puffin down to the telegraph operator in Vågen for batteries. If a strange boat came, and she feared a search, she hid the apparatus in a sack and carried it up to the potato field. Or else, if Johan was home, she sent him up into the mountains with it.

The antenna stood over the roof all through the war, since there were antennas on all the houses. When the Germans came and asked, everyone gave the same answer: the antennas are going to stay there until Norway regains her freedom.

Every evening from six-thirty to seven Magda was in her living room, listening. She heard King Haakon regret that he had had to leave the Norwegian people to themselves, and she heard Crown Princess Mærtha both promise victory and sing hymns.

Give all your burdens and your heartaches
To him who owns all of heaven's mansions,

Mærtha sang.

But there were evenings when Magda heard ugly things about

her own people, in the news from England. Sometimes, on such evenings, she went up to the loft and wept.

Getting the news around was no problem in Mostad. When Magda went with her buckets to get water in the morning, people peeked out of their windows along the way, wanting to hear if there was "anything new." Since the House Brook was the farthest point south in the Homestead, and Magda lived farthest north, she covered the whole neighborhood in one round trip. She tramped back and forth with her buckets like that and was "the voice from London" for the Mostad population.

When it was the most dramatic on the fronts, she went to the schoolteacher and borrowed a map to carry home and put on the living-room table. One evening when Johan and the boys came home from fishing with the sloop, she was standing all bent over with a kerosene lamp and was so preoccupied that she scarcely had time to look up.

At the end of the table the Philips radio was booming away, and she had a handful of straight pins. The Eighth Army had made a serious thrust at Rommel in Africa. She was sticking pins in the school map so that she could follow the report of Norwegian radio announcer Øksnevad a little better.

On the day in December that the *Scharnhorst* was sunk up at the North Cape, they were having their Christmas Festival in Mostad. With the mixed choir and dancing around the tree, and Oluf in his bridegroom's suit and shiny galoshes.

Johan had listened to the news from London before he went up to the schoolhouse, and itched to tell what he had heard. But there were strangers at the festival, and it wasn't safe to say too much.

"The Germans have had a fine defeat tonight!" he began anyway, as soon as he came inside. But then some people dragged him with them under the stairway in the entryway and told him to be quiet. "Ho, ho," Johan laughed, "I haven't said anything. I only said that the Germans have had a fine defeat tonight."

When the war was half over, Martines celebrated his eighty-seventh birthday. A couple of his boys were repairing the roof of the house one day. Then he came and positioned himself by the ladder and started to give orders about how to do things, and wanted to get up on the roof and see how they were doing up there.

His sons asked him please to stay away from there. "Don't you dare get up on the roof," they threatened him. But when they went in to get some food, and came out again to the yard, there was their father up on the roof. He stood, looking at the Homestead and the bay and the mountains all around.

That was the last time Martines showed himself out of doors. The next morning his daughter came to get Magda and said she had to come and stay, because her father was nearing the end. "Oh, Magda, how good you have been to me," he said from the pillow when she came up to him in the loft. He was giving her a receipt for all the coffee.

Later in the day, his sons who were not in Mostad came from Vågen. Martines asked that all four of them come up to the loft. They went up and stood together at the foot of the bed. Martines's failing blue eyes went from one to the other, back and forth. Then he said:

"What handsome fellows you are! Now you must get along, and hold together!"

Magda sat there that night with him. Toward morning, he had fought his way through. He was lucid until he breathed his last.

It was February and quiet snow weather the day he died. But when it was time to put him in the earth, there was a high, clear sky with frost and a brisk east wind.

Four sons carried him down to the landing. The whole Homestead followed along and sang. He had a purchased coffin from Henningsvær, with golden rosettes.

They took him in a large sloop over the bay and around Kvalnes to Nordland. The casket stood on the deck covered with a tarpaulin, and was lashed to the rail. As they rounded the point, a wave suddenly washed in over the deck. A last salt greeting from the sea on which Martines had lived his life.

On the gravestone, down by the edge of the sea, the words are carved:

The Lord Gave
And the Lord Has Taken Away
Blessed Be the Name
Of the Lord

The Avalanche

On the 25th of August, 1948, Magda stood at the shore in her travel clothes. Out at the buoy, the sloop lay with the things she was moving. When everything was ready on board, Johan came rowing in with the little dory to get her.

Then they cast off the mooring lines and set out over the bay, on a course for Vågen. It was a clear, quiet autumn day with a gentle sea. Magda sat on the forward hatch, in a black coat and red-striped wool kerchief and held her guitar in her lap. Johan's tool chest stood by the wheelhouse. It was a dull brown in color, and had metal reinforcements on all the corners. It was Magda's old wooden chest.

It had been thirty-nine years since she had come with the freighter from Å, and Johan had met her in Vågen and taken her across the bay to Mostad.

Johan had taken a job building a breakwater in Vågen. He was getting on in years, and thought about turning the sloop over to the boys. They were old enough to go to sea by themselves.

Gradually, as the boys grew up and began to go to work, Magda found herself sitting alone in the house in Mostad. Johan had always been energetic, and worked as a construction worker when he was not fishing. As the years went on, there was more and more construction work. Under those conditions, it was especially difficult to live in Mostad. When their youngest daughter offered them a room in her house in Vågen, they gratefully agreed and left.

They were not the only ones to move. The first decade after the war was the time of decision for Mostad. It began ever so small with Magda and Johan and a couple of others. Later it increased, and before the fifties were over, it was as good as empty.

It was the harbor – the one they did not get – that broke Mostad, some people said. It was the motorboats that cut the first wound into that tiny community. In 1940, Petter had to close his store; after that they were without a merchant. And that took its toll. And then the young people began gradually to move away as they formed families and began to fish in modern ways.

It was the government moving subsidy that did it, others said. After that came, things went faster and faster. Electric light poles were brought in. The most eager ones had already put up the poles outside their houses. None of them ever had lines on them. They had begun to build a road that was to tie Mostad to the rest of the island. There were a few hundred yards at each end along Nordlandshagen, and then it stopped. There were more important things to use the money for in Sørland.

And then they closed the school. That is what hurt the most. To have children without being able to have them home did not make sense.

Mostaders were like snails. When they moved, they took their houses on their backs. Took everything down neatly, lashed it onto the sloop, and ran it over to Vågen or Sørland. Almost everybody moved somewhere else on Rookery Island.

It was not a difficult day for Magda when she got into the boat. She had lived a Mostad life just like the others, and had both good and bad days on that tiny plateau at the foot of the mountain. She had not been bothered by hard work, but she had never been able to rid herself of her anxiety about the sea and the mountain.

Every time she had been about to forget, something happened again. Twenty-four useless deaths on the sea and on the mountain in the years she had lived there. It did not help that she had helped to give birth to thirty-two new Mostaders. For her, Mostad was a Hard Luck Homestead.

But there were those who thought otherwise. Petter, the shopkeeper, moved to live with a daughter in Sørland in his last years. He was one of those who had to leave early. But his heart always lay on the other side of the bay. Every day his daughter had to phone to ask what the weather was like in Mostad.

Anna was one of the last to move. She sat, completely content, in the kitchen of her unpainted house south in the Homestead and knitted and spinned, while house after house became empty around her. But finally, her legs got so that she could not live alone any longer. She moved to be with Nordis in Nordland. But as soon as spring came, she got restless and had to take a trip to Mostad and see how everything looked. She came, like a migratory bird, until the last year of her life.

★★★

The last light has gone out in the windows of Mostad. Until recently, two old people, Monrad and Katrine, were still there. They did not want to move until they were carried out. Katrine had her wish. They carried her out in a coffin. And Monrad, against his will, was moved across Mostad Bay, to live his remaining years at the home of a daughter.

Epilogue at the Fishing Hut

As this was written, Magda was ninety years old. She was a widow, in an old fisherman's cottage by the steamship dock in Vågen. She and Johan had come there twenty years earlier. It was supposed to be temporary while they remodeled their daughter's house inland on the island. But they grew to like it so well out there.

Seven years later, Johan died. Then they tried to get Magda to move. She came and stayed several weeks with her daughter. Then she packed up and moved back out again. No one could get Magda to move from the fishing hut. She could not manage to live so far inland.

"I couldn't see the ocean. That was unpleasant. But now I have it right in front of my eyes. It is beautiful, although it has done all kinds of things."

Magda lives her life both on the land and on the sea. Only half of the hut rests on solid ground. The other end stands on pilings out on the shore. When the tide is flooding and there is a little wind, Lofoten sea drives up under the planks of her floor.

A bumpy, narrow gravel road goes close by on the upper side. There is life on that road once a day, in the early evening, when the local boat is at the dock. People drift out to meet those arriving or to accompany others to the boat. Or to see whom the others are meeting or sending off.

When the local has cast loose and headed out the channel, people tramp back in again, past the walls of Magda's hut, and disappear between the fish-drying racks and the knolls farther in.

Silence settles down over the road to the dock, and silent it remains until the little hand on Magda's alarm clock has crept around the dial twice, and it again nears arrival time.

Vågen lies on the seaward side of the hut. There is life and commotion out there from the gray hours of the morning until late at night. All kinds of smacks and sloops and cutters close together, on their way to and from the fish buyer farther in. Once in a while a large sloop backs up to the wooden dock at the end of Magda's hut. That is her youngest son, Sverre, who has delivered his catch and brought his mother fresh fish for cooking.

Magda's hut is nothing special to look at. The roof has sagged down in the middle as if the king of the trolls himself had sat and ridden on it. The walls bow out, and have long since lost the red glow of a fisherman's hut. Below the window on the south wall, the white paint hangs in flakes, and only the upper windowpanes still have putty in them.

But it gleams and shines in the six wobbly old panes. And behind them the newly ironed curtains shine white. On the windowsill, geraniums sparkle a red welcome.

There are three rooms in the hut. In the end toward the sea, Magda has her chopping block and clothesline and toilet. And up toward the road there is an entry. She lives in the middle.

A rusty old key is stuck in the outer side of the entry door. It squeaks when you turn it; it is worn and nice to take hold of.

Everything smells clean, even before you actually get inside. The wooden walls of the entry are scrubbed white, and the floor is covered wall-to-wall with rag rugs. On nails along the walls, one marmalade pail after the other. There is a parade of trademarks: Løiten and Bennett and Mor Monsen, side by side. And an occasional yellow-plaid, foreign vagabond on which it says only HONEY.

Cracker boxes from Sætre stand on benches along the wall with all kinds of strange things in them. All of them have that red rooster on the outside, and all of them are arranged so that the roosters are facing the same way. A little company of roosters marching in place.

"No, now I am flustered," says Magda when you have knocked on her door and gone inside. She stands there over by the stove on the other side of the tiny room, dignified and withdrawn, in a blue, wide-striped dress. On her stomach she has an intensely red apron with white dots.

Her bewilderment does not last long. Magda has experienced too much to go around being startled. She cocks her head, claps her hands together before her, and comes lightly across the floor and offers a chair.

Magda's room is not large, but it seems so. And every little thing has its particular place, from the Bible on her nightstand to the light red plastic pot underneath.

Magda's room is four small rooms in one. Every corner is a unit by itself. First, there is the *morning room*. That is the corner with the bench and the hot plate and the china closet. Magda's day begins at the hot plate. As soon as she has stuck her feet out onto the rug-covered floor at about seven o'clock in the morning, she goes over to turn the hot plate on. While it is warming the kettle, she bends down in front of the shined-up old Mustad stove and lays in the day's first sticks of wood. And by the time she has talked nicely to old Mustad, and treated him well enough so that he crackles contentedly, the coffeepot is boiling, so that she can pour herself a cup or two of good, stiff coffee.

And then she has to keep the fire going in the stove until evening, when it is time again to pull back the flowered bedspread and crawl down into the quilts.

"I have to have a wood fire to warm myself with," Magda says. She doesn't want anything to do with electric heating. Even if it is right in the middle of the summer, she puts in a couple sticks of firewood. For the enjoyment of it. She would rather open the door to the entryway a crack if it gets too hot.

Her *dayroom* is in the southeast corner. That is where the chair stands that is near enough to old black Mustad so that it is always cozy and comfortable to sit in. And there is where the basket with the crocheting stands.

From her place, she has a view of everything that is worth seeing. Through the south window she can see the steamer dock and the breakwater and the little islands. And down along the olive brown paneled wood on the window wall she has a lot of pictures of her relatives. A half dozen children in glass and frames, and grandchildren and great-grandchildren of all ages and styles.

Magda reviews them all through her glasses when it is morning coffee break and crocheting time. There is her granddaughter in Hokksund and her grandson in Salten; there is Vera, who was taken by tuberculosis, and Bjarne, who is a gentleman in Canada. And there is her brother who *remained* on the sea.

The *evening room* is the modern room. The commode stands in that corner with the TV on top. Someone on the island loaned her the apparatus.

"It was basically a good TV. It is only the picture tube that is gone, so it is not really in bad shape."

On top of the television set there is a potted plant and a transistor radio.

"I listen to the Norwegian Top Ten when I go to bed, when I feel like it."

Magda sleeps on the side toward the ocean. The brown-painted wooden bed stands in a corner toward the southwest.

That is the *night room*. Between Magda's head and the winter storms there is only the headboard and the walls of the hut. It squeaks and creaks in the frail paneled boards when a southwester blows in.

But in the midsummers it is quite different. Then Magda lies bathed in the light of the midnight sun, and is peaceful and comfortable. The night sun shines through the north window, over the flowered oilcloth on the table and the multi-colored, rug-covered floor. For one fleeting moment the beams of the sun shine directly on the white-haired head lying on the pillow.

Sometimes Magda wakes on such nights and lies there looking at the ball of sun which fills the little window. And when the shadow crosses the pillow again, sometimes she gets up, puts on a cloak, and sits down on the bench by the south window and looks at the sea. She can sit for hours after midnight when the sun is shining and the sea is rose red.

And when she eventually decides to go to bed and sleep, she pours a cup of scalding hot coffee into herself. She knows of no better sleeping medicine.

There is a shelf over the headboard with hymn books and her reading glasses. On the wall over her bed there is a picture of Jesus, half a yard high, with a Bible passage. Magda was converted during the war. There was a missionary who went back and forth between the houses. But Magda doesn't want anything to do with all "those sects" that want people to believe as they do. She reads her Bible and travels to the state church every other Sunday in the church bus: "One can be a Christian without going and flitting around from one congregation to the other."

At the side of the red-clad Christ in the yellow frame there is a photograph in black and white. It is of Magda and Johan, both of them grinning broadly. There was a Swedish photographer who came by one time. "Put your arm around the old lady," the Swede said. So there was a picture of them grinning. Even though Johan had already had his first stroke and was a doomed man.

"He was a top-notch man, that Johan. You have to say that. He was not spineless!"

★

Magda does not go out tramping around much. If she puts on her outside clothing, it is usually to take a little trip up to the co-op. Sometimes it is months between her visits to her children on the island. But on nice evenings when the local boat has come and gone, and it has become quiet along the dock road, she might let herself out the entryway door, stick the key in the mailbox, and go for a little walk.

She might set out along the docks along the fjord to look at the boats, but she prefers to go out along the breakwater. It is a nice and flat concrete surface to walk on. And she likes to stand way out on the tip of the breakwater to see the waves play between the slippery, polished blocks of stone.

No, it is in the hut that she lives her life. She walks about all day long. Goes from one corner of the little, low-ceilinged room to the other, following the time and the light of the day. Every once in a while she goes out to the entry and clanks and rattles with the cans and baskets. Then she has to go to the shed and chop kindling. Once a day she takes the yoke down from the entryway wall and sets out along the quay with her two galvanized buckets. There is a utility sink in the hut, but she has to get water at the fish buyer's.

When evening comes she takes out a shiny brown lacquered

case from under the couch. It is no ordinary case. The whole top half is a lid. When she places the case on her lap, opens and folds the lid forward and down, she has a surface before her covered with the reddest velvet. That is Magda's writing desk. Under the velvet-covered surface there is room for a bottle of ink and a pen and old correspondence. Her brother gave her the writing desk when she was confirmed.

But mostly she reads in the evening. The *Lofoten Post* lies on the table, and the *Evangelist*; on the shelf over the headboard there are three volumes by Einar Gerhardsen, the former, long-time Labor prime minister:

"I belong to the Labor Party. That Gerhardsen is such a nice man. I have read all three of them."

On a nail in the wall over by the TV hangs a guitar with worn woodwork and a missing string. It has followed her around from the time she got it from an uncle, in Tuv, on her eighteenth birthday.

"I didn't read music. I played wild!"

But now the guitar rests. Magda's fingers have gotten too stiff. Although she has not forgotten the songs. Every year when it is time for the Old Folks Festival at the Temperance Lodge at Christmas time, they come out to her hut and ask if she will sing for the festival. Magda says no . . . but sings anyway.

It is possible to ask Magda to sing a song in the hut, too. If one does that, she twinkles and looks surprised, looks across at the rug-covered floor and says:

"No. No, that is not possible . . ."

But after a while she rises and goes over to the south window. There she takes a position with her back to you. Stands and looks through the shiny pane, over the October roses and geraniums and Christmas cactus. Looks out over the breakwater and the fjord and the lighthouse on the peninsula. Yes, if the conditions are right she can see all the way to Landegode on the other side of the fjord. And then she comes with a frail and tiny voice:

I wait the wandering moon at night
Who peeks in through the panes.
I sit here silent, all alone
And whisper long-lost names.
You lucky moon, so shining bright
Star-bright road across the night:
Look softly down, look softly down!

It shines and shines in Magda's crown of hair. She has done as St. Paul said, and he said women should not cut their hair. The last time there were scissors in her hair was eighty years before, when she was a ten-year-old girl. "And I have never used creams, or any kind of colored stuff on my mouth or in my eyebrows."

Suddenly she goes to the window again. A fishing cutter is running quietly by:

"The weather was so beautiful last night. I sat and watched the pollack seiners. It was two o'clock when I jumped into bed. Oh, can you believe how much pollack they had in their seines!"

A gust of wind rattles the walls of the fishing hut. The curtain blows behind the closed window. Magda has been promised double-paned windows for many years, but nothing ever comes of it. In the winter she fastens a shutter outside, instead. In November she goes out and hooks it in place. Then thinks the whole winter long how nice it will be when she can take the shutter down and see the ocean again.

In the dark months she sits at her loom. On the day she puts up the shutter, she sets up her loom under the light bulb that hangs from the cord from the ceiling.

"There is nothing to do but stay indoors. This is a very solid house. It howls out there among the rocks, but here . . . here I don't feel anything. The hut is fastened to the quay.

"No, now we will sip a little coffee, and then I will sing some more."

She goes to the window again and positions herself with her hands folded over her apron breast. She gropes for the melody, but soon she stops and looks at you over her shoulder:

"*Ja*, it has fine words!"

She looks again out at the fjord. But, no, once more a glance over her shoulder:

"It has three verses!"

Finally she clears her throat and begins:

It seems that I might shipwreck
when cold and storms arrive.
But when the calm has come again
I rest here, warm and live.

. . .

And now Magda rests ever. In 1985, her life came to an end. On a clear, late August morning, she died in her room at the Old People's Home. She was one hundred years old.

Until she was ninety-seven, she had refused to leave the old red fisherman's hut down by the steamship dock. She wanted to stay where she could see the ocean; where she could hear the fishing boats sailing by.

In the entry room at the municipal hall on Rookery Island

there is a framed portrait of Magda. Next to the portrait hangs the medal she received while still living in the hut: King Olav's Medal of Honor. The medal is silver, but the frame, like Magda's heart, is gold.

When Pål Espolin Johnson (b. 1940) made his publishing debut in 1972 with *Kan du trur? Epistler nordfra (Can You Believe? Epistles from the North)*, a book of letters from northern Norway, the public and the press immediately recognized a convincing, talented new author. The book went through three printings the first autumn, perhaps because it entertains while presenting a slice of the common people's cultural history. Like Johnson's later books, *Can You Believe?* creates a small monument to the heroes of ordinary work and life.

Johnson followed his initial success with *Mennesket i motgang (Human Being in Adversity*, 1973), which grew out of his dissertation about Olav Duun, one of Norway's finest authors. Duun was once considered so certain a winner of the 1925 Nobel Prize in literature that the nation's largest newspaper prematurely announced his victory on the front page; the prize went to George Bernard Shaw instead. The theme of that study is how a human being can bear an unusually heavy burden through life but still persevere, how one can grow through adversity while others give up or become bitter.

For Love of Norway (Alt for Norge [literally, 'All for Norway'], 1975) is Johnson's first book in English translation and the one he considers his best. It is yet another tribute to both ordinary people and perseverance in the face of adversity and was an immediate success the whole length of the country, a significant achievement in itself. Regionalism is strong in Norway, but Johnson, although born and reared in southern Norway, used his experiences as a deckhand on a coastal express boat traveling from Bergen to the Russian border and as an assistant sheriff in the far north to overcome regionalism and produce a book that is honest, sensitive, and true to the reality of an outlying fishing village, Mostad. His success is noted by the northern newspaper *Vesterålen*, which pronounced that *For Love of Norway* contains 'the joy and art of storytelling at its best. . . . It is delightful for us northerners and coastal people to find our past and our story told so honestly and beautifully by someone from the outside [i.e., the south]. . . . He lets people be as they are, strong and robust, chiseled by the hard and unyielding existence of the settlement . . . people who confront death with clenched fists, who grimly battle storms at sea to the very end, but who, when the fight is over, thank God for every day they have had, and who sing the dead to their graves' (December 1, 1975).

Uniting Norwegian opinion is just one of the book's achievements. A more significant one is that reached by all good documentary fiction. *For Love of Norway* subjects fact to creative intelligence to capture a moment of history for us as few historians could. The conversations in this book have not been tape-recorded, yet we hear them as if they were; none of the story was directly observed, but we experience it as if the author had been present every moment. The facts of Mostad are those that only a keen and sympathetic artist can report, not just from his notes, but from care and an inner identification with those whose stories he tells.

Johnson uses three important techniques to make Mostad as alive and objectively real as it appears in his book. The first is a simple, spare style that suggests both the ruggedness of the life he describes and the language of the people whose story he relates. There are, for example, very few complex sentences in *For Love of Norway* and even fewer latinate words. The second is a regular juxtaposition of simple symbols to profound events, a technique that replicates the world view of the fishing village and thwarts any tendency to romanticize Mostad. This occurs, for example, when Bernt and Johan drown at sea, and the second of the two brothers is carried to his mother's kitchen as the boys' father sits on a rock by the sea. The mother covers her son's face with a small cloth and then, as the boy would have himself, she puts his boots by the fire to dry. It occurs again when Nordis, embarassed by the worn flag she carries, learns of the death of her brother and father at sea. All the tragedy of her poverty and dashed hopes is captured in the image of the tattered flag that she trails on the ground. And the third technique is Johnson's consistently objective stance, like that of a photographer. The camera of Johnson's mind records everything, seemingly without comment or censure. Thus we come to know and even appreciate Maren, Magda's tyrannical mother-in-law, as much as we appreciate and know the wonderfully alive and compelling Magda herself. We are left ultimately with a portrait of past individuals, of a village and social system fast disappearing. And in that portrait, of course, we find a reflection, sometimes comforting, sometimes disturbing, of ourselves.

Northern Norway appears in the two books that follow *For Love of Norway*, and this time Johnson accompanies the texts with a wealth of his own photographs. *Hurtigruta (Steamships)*, a book about the express boats that ply Norway's coastal waters, was among the country's best-sellers in 1978. Its color and black-and-white photographs bring to life the people on and along the route in Norway's harsh, stunningly beautiful landscape. *Steam-*

ships shows the relationship of the past to the present, for the *hurtigrute*, a fleet of a particular kind of ship, represents a whole way of life that comes from the Norwegians' Viking history and what they have known and been for a thousand years. *Norge – mitt Nord-Norge* (*Norway – My Northern Norway*, 1983), likewise richly illustrated with Johnson's own photographs, takes the reader on a spellbinding tour of the northernmost part of Norway, from Helgeland to the Russian border. With characteristic warmth and insight, Johnson details the lives of his countrymen who people the land of the summer midnight sun. Both *Norway – My Northern Norway* and *Steamships* have been reprinted several times.

In his most recent book, Johnson turns his attention to the American Midwest, an area he came to know when he was a visiting scholar at Luther College in Decorah, Iowa, from 1984 to 1985. *Amerika-brev* (*Letters from America*, 1985), a compilation of the letters that Johnson started writing to a Norwegian newspaper shortly after his arrival in Decorah, chronicles his sojourn in America and presents us with yet another picture of ourselves. Again he approaches his subject with a photographer's eye; again he portrays his characters with sensitive objectivity; and again we are drawn to a particular historical period and place as if it were precisely our own. The same artistic vision that brought forth Mostad has brought forth small sketches of Norwegian America in Decorah and the Midwest for future generations. In the story of Mostad and Magda (the latter of whom had died by the time the last three paragraphs of the epilogue were written for the English translation) an American audience now can see the special talent that Johnson brings to his literary work. All of that work, it is clear, was produced for an enduring love of Norway.

Other volumes in the series
Modern Scandinavian Literature
in Translation include:

Knut Faldbakken, *Adam's Diary*
Translated by Sverre Lyngstad

Jan Fridegård, *Land of Wooden Gods*
Translated by Robert E. Bjork

P. C. Jersild, *Children's Island*
Translated by Joan Tate

P. C. Jersild, *House of Babel*
Translated by Joan Tate

Christer Kihlman, *The Blue Mother*
Translated by Joan Tate

Dea Trier Mørch, *Evening Star*
Translated by Joan Tate

Dea Trier Mørch, *Winter's Child*
Translated by Joan Tate

Villy Sørensen, *The Downfall of the Gods*
Translated by Paula Hostrup-Jessen

Villy Sørensen, *Tutelary Tales*
Translated by Paula Hostrup-Jessen

August Strindberg, *The Roofing
Ceremony* and *The Silver Lake*
Translated by David Mel Paul and
Margareta Paul

Henrik Tikkanen, *The Thirty Years'
War* Translated by George Blecher
and Lone Thygesen Blecher